Ambition

Why it's good to want
more and how to get it

Rachel Bridge

CAPSTONE
A Wiley Brand

For Harry and Jack

Contents

Introduction

"Intelligence without ambition is
a bird without wings."
Salvador Dali

When you are a child, adults are always asking you what you want to be when you grow up. Along with "What's your favourite subject at school?" and "Haven't you grown!" it is pretty much the standard question at any family gathering and indeed sometimes used by teachers as a lesson theme. I can still vividly remember a fabulous picture painted by my sister at the age of five, depicting her as a pop star with sparkly purple hair and big red shoes.

As you get older, however, people gradually stop asking you what you want to do, and by the time you are grown up no one ever asks at all. Presumably they feel that you have either already achieved what you wanted to in life, or you haven't, in which case you probably don't particularly want to talk about it.

It is a real shame because no matter what you have already achieved and regardless of what stage you are at in life, having the ambition to achieve more can be a wonderful, life-affirming force. Ambition drives us on to better and greater things, whether for ourselves, for our family, or for the world. Without it we would have no progress, no inventions, no innovation, and no change for the better.

Unfortunately, the concept of ambition is often misunderstood and as a result can sometimes be regarded with suspicion. People who are old enough to remember the 1980s, in particular, recall how wanting more somehow became synonymous with shouty people with big hair wearing red braces or shoulder pads. Ambition became a dirty word, a shorthand term for greed and the desire to win at all costs.

Even now, many of the words used to describe ambition are harsh, fierce words – burning, raw, naked, ruthless ambition, anyone?

So let's start by clarifying exactly what we mean by ambition. At its simplest, ambition is the desire to make the most of your potential to achieve something special, which would make a profound difference to your life and to those of others, whether that be through success, achievement or distinction. That might mean the desire to create something unique; reach the top of your field; start a business; become an expert in a particular area; or make a positive difference to the world.

Ambition spells the difference between those who are content to let random circumstance determine their journey through life, and those who would like to have a say in where they end up.

The late American preacher Dr Myles Munroe divided opinion with some of the views he held, but he got it right when he talked about the tragedy of people not using their potential.

He said: "The wealthiest places in the world are not the gold mines of South America or the oil fields of Iraq or Iran. They are not the diamond mines of South Africa or the banks of the world. The wealthiest place on the planet is just down the road. It is the cemetery. There lie buried companies that were never started, inventions that were never made, best-selling books that were never written, and masterpieces that were never painted. In the cemetery is buried the greatest treasure of untapped potential."

Or as one of the people I interviewed for this book put it: "It's about trying to squeeze the juice out of life."

The interesting thing about ambition is that it is not just a driver for success; it can actually increase your chances of being successful. A study of more than 700 people with high ability by American academics Timothy Judge and John Kammeyer-Meyer in 2012 found there was a definite positive link between ambition and success. In particular, they discovered a link between ambition and educational attainment and prestige, which in turn led to higher wages, more prestigious work, and greater satisfaction with life. In other words, your ambition will not just set you on the road to success; it will also increase your chances of reaching your ultimate goal.

The purpose of this book is to show you how to use your ambition to achieve the big goals in your life. It will show you how to harness and direct your ambition in the most effective way, how to target it to overcome the things that stand in the way of your goals, how to chart your progress, how to stay motivated. And above all, how to succeed.

All the advice in this book is based on the stories and experiences of successful people in all walks of life and is grounded in academic research and proven studies.

The world is an exciting place, full of wonderful possibilities and amazing opportunities. And the good news is that whatever ultimate goal you have in mind, your ambition can help you get there. Faster.

So what are you waiting for?

1

Be clear about what you are trying to achieve

"You have brains in your head. You have feet in your shoes. You can steer yourself any direction you choose."

Dr Seuss

Goals can come in all shapes and sizes. So before you start, you need to be very clear in your mind about where you are trying to get to. What do you really want to do? Become a best-selling novelist? Be promoted to a high-flying role at work? Build a school in a poor underdeveloped part of the world? Start your own business? Win a gold medal at the next Olympic Games? Get to the top of your academic field? Be a professional deep-sea diver? Whatever it is, if you are going to successfully use your ambition to achieve your ultimate goal, you need to have a very strong sense of where you are heading before you begin. Otherwise you will get lost long before you reach your destination.

By taking the time now to think hard about what your ambition looks like, you can dramatically improve your chances of success before you even start. Just make sure your ambition has these six essential ingredients:

1. Your ambition should be big
2. Your ambition should be measurable
3. Your ambition should be personal
4. Your ambition should make a difference

5. Your ambition should be achievable

6. Your ambition should be something you really, really want to do

Let's look at each of these in turn:

1. Your ambition should be big

It may sound counter-intuitive but having a big ambition actually improves your chances of success. If the ultimate goal you are trying to achieve is too small, it can be easy to feel that you don't need to make much of an effort to achieve it. Which invariably means that you don't make any effort at all. So inevitably, nothing changes. And your ultimate goal never gets reached.

If, on the other hand, you have set yourself a big challenging goal, then if you are to have any chance of achieving it at all, you know you must face it head on and be fully prepared. And leave nothing to chance because it is going to take every ounce of your focus and energy to even have a shot at getting anywhere close to it.

In the 1960s, American psychologist Professor Edwin Locke did a lot of pioneering research into the link between goal setting and performance. After reviewing a decade's worth of laboratory and field studies, he found that in 90% of cases, setting specific and challenging goals led to higher performance than setting easy goals or "do your best" goals. He concluded that the more difficult a goal is, the harder people will work to achieve it.

This is why people might successfully build a house from scratch when they have never even put together a flat-pack bookcase, or run a marathon when they have never found the motivation to join a gym. Big becomes easier to achieve because it sits itself right in your sight line and flatly refuses to budge until you do something about it.

There is a wonderful children's story by Jack Kent called *There's No Such Thing as a Dragon*. It is about a small boy called Billy who finds a small dragon at the end of his bed when he wakes up one morning. He goes to tell his mother about it, but she refuses to admit that the dragon is real, even as she cleans the house around it, climbing in and out of windows because the dragon is in the way. So the dragon grows and grows and grows, until it has grown so big that it walks off with the house attached to it. It is only when the postman has to chase after it down the street and Billy's father has to climb up the dragon's back to get into the house, that his mother is finally forced to acknowledge its existence. "Why did it have to grow so big?" she asks. "I'm not sure," says Billy, "but I think it just wanted to be noticed."

Make sure your ambition is big enough for you to notice it.

Remember, if nobody laughs at your idea and tells you that you must be mad to even think of trying to do it, you are setting your sights too low. Much too low. Any successful person will tell you that at some point in their lives, probably more than once, someone has quietly taken them to one side and told them firmly to give up their ambition because they will never succeed at it. If everyone nods their head in approval and tells you what a great idea it is, you are doing it all wrong.

2. Your ambition should be measurable

Every weekend in Scotland, dozens of enthusiastic climbers set out to pursue an activity known as Munro-bagging. This is the act of climbing a Munro, the name given to the 282 highest mountains in Scotland over 3000 feet. They are named after Sir Hugh Munro, a Scottish mountaineer who first catalogued them back in 1891. It is possible to bag several Munros at a time, or even to try and tick them all off in one go – the current record for climbing them all in one continuous round is just under 40 days.

It is an immensely popular activity, and with good reason. That's because goals are much more satisfying to achieve when you can measure them. Whichever Munro you choose to bag, you've either climbed the mountain, or you haven't. There is no middle way and no room for doubt. (Check out www.munromagic.com or www.walkhighlands.co.uk/munros for more information if this sort of thing interests you.)

The fact is people are more likely to achieve their goals if they are measurable, simply because they are easier to see, and easier to aim for. And because you know for sure when you have got there.

3. Your ambition should be personal

When he was a child, Edward Peppitt fell in love with light-houses. He says: "My love of lighthouses came from holidays spent at my grandma's house. I had the attic bedroom, and the lighthouse at Dungeness nearby flashed through my bedroom window and lit up my bedroom wall. Aged about six, that left quite an impression. It made me want to stop and look at lighthouses on other holidays, which in turn led me to want to visit them all."

As he grew older, Edward promised himself that one day he would cycle around England and Wales, visiting the 203 working and former lighthouses built along the coastline. But work and family commitments meant he never quite got round to doing his trip. Then in 2012 at the age of 43 he was diagnosed with relapsing-remitting multiple sclerosis, a debilitating condition that caused him to go temporarily blind for three months and his legs to go numb. Edward, who ran a publishing business, also had chronic fatigue, which left him unable to work, and debts started to mount up. He says: "It never crossed my mind that things would ever be the same again. I was in complete denial for six months and hit rock bottom."

Fortunately Edward discovered Shift MS, a social network and support community for people with the disease. With their support he realized that just because he had MS it did not mean he had to give up on life, or indeed on his long-held ambition of visiting the lighthouses. So he started training three times a week, cycling 15–20 miles each time and in May 2015 set off on his 3500 mile journey, with the additional aim of raising £25,000 for Shift MS. As well as the lighthouses on the mainland, he planned to visit the islands, including the Isle of Wight, the Scilly Isles, Lundy and the Channel Islands, and beg for ferry crossings and fishing fleets to visit the rock lighthouses too. Much of the trip was over rough and inhospitable terrain and Edward nearly gave up several times, overwhelmed by the rain and wind and the loss of his iPhone. He also missed his three children. But he kept going and three months later achieved his ultimate goal. You can see his journey at www.thebeaconbike.co.uk.

Edward is clear about why he undertook such a huge challenge. He says: "I spent a lot of time at charity coffee mornings, where lots of people with MS would sit around a table and moan about their latest symptoms. I hated that. So if I have achieved anything, it's to demonstrate that MS does not mean a life sentence of ill health. One may need to make compromises, but someone with MS can still achieve pretty much anything they want to. I want people with long term conditions to be inspired and stay positive."

He adds: "It is not about weathering the elements, it is about a personal challenge. Life goes on. Just make the most of every day."

4. Your ambition should be achievable

One of the main reasons people don't achieve their ambitions is because their ambitions are unrealistic. If your ultimate goal doesn't have any chance of becoming reality, you will be wasting your time. If you are over 30 and still dreaming of becoming a professional footballer, for instance, it is time to find a new goal.

Don't set yourself up for failure by letting your ambitions get bigger than your abilities. Your ultimate goal has to be attainable otherwise you are just kidding yourself.

You also need to avoid goals that depend on the actions of others – or which require technical advancements beyond that which you can achieve yourself. Otherwise you will not only set yourself up for immense frustration as you wait for someone to get on with inventing or creating the thing you need, you will also give yourself the perfect excuse for procrastinating indefinitely.

Ask yourself:

> Does your age, height or other physical characteristics make your goal impossible?
>
> Is there a certain level of natural talent you absolutely need to have in order to achieve your goal?
>
> Does someone else need to invent something or create something before you can achieve your goal?

If the answer to any of the above is yes, you may need to think again.

The good news, however, is that even if your ultimate goal in its current state is unrealistic, it may be possible to tweak it until it becomes a goal you could achieve. Even if you don't meet the criteria to be accepted into a top international ballet school, you could still start a dance company of your own. Look at your goal carefully and consider if there might be a plan B. There is often more than one way to get to the top of a mountain.

5. Your ambition should make a difference

When Alan Barnes, a frail disabled pensioner, was attacked outside his home in Gateshead and broke his collarbone, Katie Cutler, a 21-year-old beautician who didn't know him but read about his story in the newspaper, set up a fundraising page for him in support. She wrote on the page: "Alan is too frightened to return to his home so with the help of his sister he's looking for new accommodation. I'm trying to raise £500 for Alan, which will help him towards the cost of relocating, in order for him to feel safe and carry on with his life. I was so upset that anyone could target a disabled pensioner and be so cruel. We can't take away what has happened but with a little donation we can make the future a prettier one and help towards the cost of his new home. Thank you all."

Katie initially hoped to raise £500, but as donations poured in from around the world, she ended up raising £330,000, enough to buy Alan a new house. People got in touch to offer practical help too, from building work to legal advice.

Katie has now set up a charitable foundation (www.katiecutlerfoundation.co.uk) to raise money for other worthy causes. In 2015 she was awarded a British Empire Medal by the Queen in recognition of her achievements.

The best kinds of goals are the ones that make a real difference – to your life, to the life of others. They are the kinds of goals that push you to the limit of your capabilities and beyond, which in the process change you and those around you for the better. If it doesn't much matter to you or anyone else whether you achieve your ultimate goal or not, the chances are you never will, because there will never be that sense of urgency driving you forward.

6. It should be something you really, really want to do

Think about what you really want out of life. What is it? The whole point about ambition – and indeed life – is that it's yours. It belongs to you and no one else. Don't ever fall into the trap of trying to achieve someone else's goal. Life is too short. It is so easy to do, particularly if it is your parents' dream and you want to please them and make them happy. But if your goal doesn't make you want to leap out of bed in the morning or sing in the shower, forget about it. You have to want to do it, a lot. Because otherwise you will give up before you get there. Half-hearted won't work.

Michael Hayman is the co-founder, with Nick Giles, of Seven Hills, a campaign consultancy that has won many awards. He also co-founded the StartUp Britain campaign to encourage entrepreneurship in the UK. Michael has also made no secret of the fact that he wants to grow his business to be as successful and influential as Saatchi & Saatchi, which was the world's largest advertising agency in the 1980s.

Michael says that having a clear goal has been hugely important to him: "The very best advice I was ever given was from a head-hunter who told me, you have got to start at the end and work back, because if you know where you want to finish up, the journey becomes much easier. That was a real Damascus moment for me. Because until that point I had a sort of ill-directed ambition that I wanted to do something, and to be someone, but I really had no idea about where I wanted it to take me."

Knowing the end goal has helped him to stay focused, he says: "When it was just the two of us, buying furniture in Ikea for our office, the goal felt like a long way away. There I was, pontificating away to Nick about how we were going to be the next Saatchi, and the next moment, I was saying, do you think we will be able to put this desk together? But we have a very clear ambitious goal. I want to build the best. I want the best team, the best company. And I have a sense of what the journey might be, and how it all fits together."

This focus has also given Michael the confidence to make bold choices. At Seven Hills he has introduced a concept called Project Unsackable, which, he says, "is all the mad ideas we have which would have got us sacked in someone else's company". The ideas this has generated have already become key chapters in the company's history – the StartUp Britain campaign, the MADE festival for entrepreneurs held in Sheffield every year, and now a book, *Mission: How the Best in Business Break Through*, which sets out the company's campaigning purpose.

Michael says: "One of the proudest moments of my life was seeing the StartUp Britain bus go round the country. I remember turning up in Nottingham and seeing people queueing down the street to get on it."

Goals are good. Make sure yours is clear enough to see.

Over to You

1. Write down your ultimate goal on a piece of paper and date it.

2. Now study it carefully. Is it big enough for you to really get excited about? Is it realistic enough for you to think you could achieve it?

3. List three ways in which achieving your goal would improve your life or the lives of others.

"Ambition beats genius 99% of the time."

Jay Leno, US comedian and talkshow host

2

Make room in your life for your ambition

"It is our choices, Harry, that show what we truly are, far more than our abilities."
Professor Dumbledore, Harry Potter and the Chamber of Secrets, *JK Rowling*

I f you are serious about achieving your ultimate goal, you need to make space for it. Sounds obvious, doesn't it, but in reality the reason why so many people fail to reach their goal is they tack it on as an afterthought. They never consciously make room for it, and so it quickly gets lost amongst all the other things going on in their lives.

When you begin a new relationship with someone, get a pet or have a baby, you have to quickly work out how they will fit into your life. It is no different with goals. You have to put it right at the heart of what you do each day and if need be rearrange the rest of your life around it. You have to make it a priority. That doesn't mean neglecting all the other important elements of your life such as your family, friends and job, but it does mean finding a way in which they can all peacefully coexist.

Here's how:

1. Create a supportive environment for your goal

The environment you put yourself in will have an enormous impact on whether or not you achieve your goal. At a very basic level, this means that if you want to improve your chances of becoming a champion skier, you should live in a country that has top-quality ski facilities and snow for much of the year. If you want to be a professional surfer, you should move to Cornwall – or Hawaii. If you want to start an internet company and be the next dot com millionaire, you should consider getting shared office space in one of the Tech City clusters set up around the country. Back in the 1870s and 1880s, if you wanted to be an impressionist painter, you should have headed straight for the Paris Left Bank and started exhibiting your work in the Salon des Refusés alongside Monet, Cezanne, Degas and Renoir.

That's because achieving your goal will be a hundred times easier if you can create an environment where your goal feels right at home. Where it makes more sense to achieve it than not.

This is why start-up businesses dramatically improve their survival rates when surrounded by other start-up businesses, and why far-sighted support organizations create geographical clusters and incubator space for them. When everyone else around you is creating amazing impressionist paintings/internet start-ups/world record downhill skiing times, your big existential dilemma very quickly switches from "Should I be doing this?" to "Why on earth didn't I do this five years ago?"

You also need to make the right lifestyle choices that support your goal on a practical level. Rhian Rosario, 23, is the current female World Kickboxing Champion, the highest accolade possible in the sport. Rhian started kickboxing at the age of 14 and trains intensively four times a week, as well as taking part in competitions at weekends. To make all that possible she works at a sports centre in Swansea, where the managers understand her goal and are happy to support it.

Rhian says: "I compete regularly and I need to train for it. When I started working at the leisure centre I told the managers that I would need to have quite a few weekends off to take part in competitions. I also wouldn't be able to work some evenings because that is when I train. They were happy to let me do that and said they would support me going forward, which they have."

Rhian says having the time and freedom to be able to train properly and enter every competition has made a huge difference to her success in the sport, not least because it has enabled her to improve her fighting technique. She says: "I used to rush it, I would just jump on the mat and get the fight over with. I wasn't thinking of the strategy of how to win the fight, I was more concerned about doing the fight. Slowing down the fight is definitely working for me."

If you can't afford to surround yourself with like-minded people on a permanent basis, doing it on a short-term basis can be a real tonic too. Time spent in the company of people who see the world in the same way as you do can be immensely restorative. Here are some ideas:

- Look for relevant talks and events in your area. If your goal involves going on an exploration trip somewhere, the Royal Geographical Society (www.rgs.org) holds lectures every Monday night for its members. A typical evening – "Explorer Levison Wood will be speaking about his nine-month expedition walking the length of the Nile through six countries; encountering civil war, close calls with crocodiles and much more." Membership is open to anyone for an annual fee and if you are not near London you can watch the lectures online instead.

- Escape the City (www.escapethecity.org) is a global online community of people who have escaped, or who are looking to escape, unfulfilling jobs and careers in the corporate world for more meaningful ones in the non-corporate world. The organization runs 15-week career change courses in remote parts of the world through its Escape School, holds worldwide meetup events and provides an online chat forum on their website for members.

- Volunteer organizations can be a great low-cost way of being in the company of like-minded people. World Wide Opportunities on Organic Farms (www.wwoof.net) enables volunteers to work on organic farms around the world for a few days or weeks in return for food, accommodation and the opportunity to learn about organic lifestyles.

- Go online. There are internet forums for all kinds of interests and passions. Sign up to the ones you like the sound of and observe for a while to see if the topics and tone are relevant to you.

2. Create dedicated physical space for your project

This could be a study, spare room, garage, shed – whatever you have available. My ability to work at home has been transformed since I asked a local builder to put up an internal wall to divide the front room and create a study of my own. All my things in one place, all the time, instead of floating around the house getting lost and forming piles of random papers and general chaos. Bliss. It doesn't have to be big or grand but if you can find a place in your home that you can make your own and close the door on, grab it. If you can't, then find a corner of your own and buy lots of plastic boxes with lids to keep everything in one place.

Another option is to rent the space you need. If you need to store a lot of things, you could rent a self-storage unit – anything from the size of a small cupboard to a walk-in room, depending on how much space you require. If you need to hold meetings away from the home, several providers offer temporary office or meeting room space, which you can hire by the hour in a location to suit you. If you need land, garages or commercial property, you can rent them too.

When it comes to actually working on your project then it is hard to beat using your home as a base, simply because it is so handy and costs nothing. But you do need to be careful not to be distracted by washing up, unmade beds, DIY jobs to be finished, children's toys to be tidied away. Be ruthless and train yourself to focus only on the task you have set yourself. Three tips:

1. Close doors. If you can't see the dirty dishes or piles of unwashed clothes, you are less likely to feel the need to do something about them.

2. Leave a note. If you live in a place where people are always popping round to have a chat, try pinning a note to the door and asking visitors to only come round at certain times.

3. If possible, choose the room where you are least likely to be led astray by the things around you. You might prefer to avoid the kitchen if you are the type of person who will be jumping up every five minutes to make a cup of tea and a pile of buttered toast. Then again you might prefer to avoid the living room if you think you would be tempted to put the television on in the background. If there is nothing in the room to distract you, you will get a lot more done.

3. Create space in your head for your project

Sometimes it can be hard to focus on what you need to be doing, simply because your head is so full of other things. You may have to consciously clear a space in your mind for it.

Hugh Rycroft had developed a successful career as a comedy writer. He had worked his way up from devising sketches for the satirical radio show *Week Ending* to writing for shows such as *Light Lunch* and *Friends Like These* with Ant and Dec. He even wrote jokes for Clive James and Bob Monkhouse.

But as Hugh learnt more about how the industry worked, he realized that what he really wanted to do was create formats for television quiz shows. He says: "It hadn't really occurred to me that people got paid to invent game shows. And when it did occur to me, I thought I would be quite good at it because I like games and I have a logical streak that runs through my thinking, which is quite important. That was when I thought, I can do that."

But because comedy writing requires a high degree of intense concentration, Hugh realized he needed to create space in his head to be able to think up new television shows. So he took action. He says: "I frequently turned comedy writing work down. I became known as the writer who doesn't want to write."

It was a brave move. Trying to earn a living selling ideas for new television shows is an extremely precarious thing to do and indeed for many years Hugh earned hardly any money: "There were whole years at a time when for all the difference it would have made, I could have been on holiday. For about three years in a row I earned less than £5000."

He eventually had some success with a quiz show called *School's Out*, which was presented by comedian Danny Wallace. Then came the big one – a quiz show called *Tipping Point*, which involves a giant version of the coin cascade machine found in amusement arcades. *Tipping Point* has gone on to be a huge success, clocking up hundreds of episodes. Hugh now also has a new show on television, *Decimate*, and has set up his own production company, Mighty.

Creating the space to focus on his goal has also unexpectedly given Hugh something else. He says: "I think, by chance or by accident, this might well be the thing I am best at."

4. Build it into your regular routine

One of the simplest ways of making room for your ultimate goal is to make it part of your daily routine, so that you are working towards it almost without noticing. This also takes away the effort of wondering whether to do it, or when, or how.

If you want to learn Chinese commit to learning ten new characters each day over breakfast. If you want to become a best-selling novelist, commit to writing 500 words every morning before work.

The great thing about this approach is it doesn't rely on you being enthusiastic or in the right frame of mind, because the trigger to do the new thing comes from your routine not your level of motivation or willpower. As the ancient Greek philosopher Aristotle said, "We are what we repeatedly do. Excellence, therefore, is not an act, but a habit."

5. Get organized

If you have ever found yourself standing on the doorstep, staring into the middle distance, trying to remember what it is you have forgotten, you are not alone. Most of us spend our days in a blur of disorganization, wasting enormous amounts of time looking for keys, mobile phones, sunglasses and credit cards.

Now is the time to put an end to this and get organized once and for all. Not only will your life function more effectively, you will also feel happier and more in control of your life. And that will help you stay totally focused on achieving your ambition.

This is how to do it:

- After talking to someone on the phone about your project, immediately email them to thank them for their time and to confirm what you have just spoken about and what action you both plan to take. Nothing complicated – just a quick "Hi Nick, it was great to speak to you just now about taking a stand at your next conference. I will get in touch with Maria to discuss logistics, as you suggest, and look forward to receiving a price list from you." Not only is it polite and quick to do, it is also a really easy way of keeping track of when conversations took place, with whom and why. Then whenever you need it, you can just search for the email and if need be forward it to others. Brilliantly quick, simple and free.

- Photograph everything. Use a smartphone or digital camera to snap everything from passports and signs to documents and venues. One person I know even photographs business cards every time they are given one. Recording everything like this means that if you suddenly need information, you are very likely to already have it with you. Your phone or camera will even tag each photo with the date and time it was taken.

- Plan the next day. Before you go to bed, locate and retrieve everything you are going to need tomorrow and put it somewhere prominent, ideally by the front door. Yes, basic common sense, but how many of us do it? Start now.

- Have a small selection of coordinated outfits that are suitable for meetings and other formal occasions, and make sure they are always clean and ready to wear. That way you can quickly grab one without having to think about whether everything matches.

Finally, don't mistake getting organized for doing the goal itself. Think back to when you were at school – making an elaborate exam revision timetable using highlighter pens and coloured stickers may have been fun but it was not actually the same as revising, no matter how great it looked. In the same way, creating a detailed training schedule to become an Ironman athlete is all very well, but if you don't actually do the training it is worthless.

Over to You

1. Walk around your home. Where are you going to establish the base for achieving your goal?

2. Now take the first steps towards making this happen right now – get a desk and chair, put up a whiteboard to scribble ideas on, buy a set of pens.

3. Declutter your wardrobe. Keep the clothes that make you feel positive, strong and in control, and give the rest to charity.

"It always seems impossible until it's done."

Nelson Mandela

3
Make a plan

"A goal without a plan is just a wish."
Antoine de Saint-Exupery

In the 1970s there was a hugely popular comedy series on television called *The Good Life*. It followed the fictional exploits of Tom and Barbara Good, a married couple who decided to turn their backs on conventional modern life and try to become self-sufficient by growing their own food and keeping livestock. The comic twist was that instead of living in the countryside, they lived in a suburban semi-detached house in Surrey.

They planted fruit and vegetables in their garden and got some chickens and pigs, a goat and a cockerel. They made their own clothes and even tried to generate their own electricity from animal waste, their attempts watched with bafflement and occasionally exasperation by their more conventional neighbours, Margot and Jerry. However, it quickly became clear that Tom and Barbara didn't really know what they were doing – and so were fairly hopeless at it. The pig kept escaping, their homemade bread tasted horrible, and their methane-powered car continually broke down.

All of which made for very funny television, but is less than ideal in real life. If you are going to pursue an ambition, you need to think about how you are actually going to make it work in practice. You need to make a plan.

The fact is, without a plan, your goal is likely to remain just that. A goal.

A few years ago Dr Gail Matthews at the Dominican University in Illinois conducted a study of 149 people from a variety of backgrounds, professions, levels and sectors to determine the exact link between plans and goals. She randomly divided the respondents into five groups with increasing levels of commitment, as follows:

- Group 1 had to think about their goals for the next four weeks but not write them down.
- Group 2 had to write down their goals.
- Group 3 had to write down their goals and also commit to specific actions aimed at taking them closer to their goal.
- Group 4 had to do all of this plus share them with a friend.
- Group 5 had to do everything group 4 had to do, plus send a weekly progress report to a friend.

After four weeks Dr Matthews discovered that the group who wrote down their goals were significantly more likely to have achieved them within the allotted time frame than those who didn't write them down. And that the greater the level of commitment required, shown by undertaking specific goal-directed actions, the more likely the goals would be achieved. The people in group 1 only achieved 43% of their stated goals. The people in group 2 achieved 67% of their stated goals, while the people in group 5 achieved 76% of their goals: almost twice as much as the people in group 1.

How you actually create your plan is up to you. Some people love making fancy PowerPoint presentations and creating elaborate pie charts and spreadsheets. Others don't. That's fine too. A scribbled note on a side of A4 will work just as well. Just make sure you do write it down.

Here's how to make a plan that will actually work:

1. Include everything you need to think about

This might be:

- **Aims.** It is a good idea to remind yourself why you are doing this.

- **Skills and training.** What kind of skills and training are you going to need? How and where are you going to acquire these?

- **Experience.** What additional experience are you going to need? How and where will you get this?

- **Resources.** What additional resources are you going to need – equipment, premises, practical help, transport?

- **Budget.** All of the above is likely to cost money. How much will it cost and where will you get the money?

- **External input.** What kind of help and advice are you likely to need from other people? How will you go about getting this?

- **Logistics.** What adjustments are you going to need to make in your own life in order to make your goal possible – will you have to give up your job, move house, change countries?

- **Time scale.** How long is this all going to take? When do you realistically hope to achieve your goal?

The great thing is that by putting everything into your plan, it also becomes a useful document to show people who may want to help you. If you need advice, mentoring, sponsorship, investment, or even just a travelling companion to come with you on your adventures, having a ready-made plan to hand will be immensely helpful.

2. Specify exactly what you plan to do and when you plan to do it

This is a big one. It is far more effective to decide to get up at 6am every day to practise some scales than it is to simply decide you want to become a world-class trumpet player. That's because it is much harder to wriggle out of doing something when you've tied it to a specific action at a specific time.

In a study published in the *British Journal of Health Psychology* in 2002 looking at what encourages people to exercise, researchers found that motivation was much less important than intention. The survey of 248 people, which was conducted by Sarah Milne from Bath University, Sheina Orbell from Essex University and Paschal Sheeran from Sheffield University, measured how frequently people exercised over a two-week period. One group of people were asked to read a pamphlet on the benefits of exercise for reducing the risk of heart disease; the other group were also asked to read the same pamphlet, but in addition were asked to make a plan setting up when and where they would exercise.

The difference in outcome was astounding. In the motivation group of people who only read the pamphlet, 35% of participants exercised at least once a week. However, in the intention group of people who read the pamphlet and also made a plan of when they would exercise an astonishing 91% of participants exercised at least once a week. In other words, simply by writing down a plan which set out exactly when and where they intended to exercise, the people in the second group were much more likely to do it – between two and three times as much, in fact.

And this study is not an isolated case. Other studies have also come to the same conclusion; that stating when and where you intend to do something will take you closer to your goal.

3. Tell someone what you are doing

If you tell someone about your goals, you are more likely to achieve them. This is partly because it makes your goal more real once you have said it out loud. And partly because it gets really embarrassing if you have to come up with excuses every time you bump into them about why you haven't done anything about achieving it yet. Basically, the higher the likelihood of someone asking you repeatedly if you have done something yet, the greater the chance of you actually doing it – if only to shut them up.

4. Set deadlines

Even for the most disciplined person, a project can easily drift off into the clouds without deadlines to tie it down. The good news is there are lots of handy ways to make this easy for you. Significant birthdays, holidays and other family events can be great motivators to achieve a particular milestone because they come with their own built-in countdown to the big day. Plus the fear of spoiling the occasion if you don't achieve it. It is amazing how the prospect of walking down the aisle, for example, can turn a hopeless dieter into a really good one.

External events are fantastic motivators too, so build them into your plan as much as you can. A goal of running a marathon can be broken down into a series of local 5k and 10k runs throughout the year, which naturally builds up towards the big run itself. For people with school-age children, the entire year is helpfully broken up into a series of deadlines to hit – half terms, school holidays, the start of a new school term, a new school year. Use them to structure your project.

Arranging a meeting to discuss or present something you haven't yet created can work wonders too. That can really get the motivation – and the adrenalin – pumping. If you are feeling really brave you can also announce plans via social media or on your website.

5. Rearrange the furniture

This one is harsh but effective. If you have a tendency to spend your evenings slumped in front of the television instead of getting on with useful things that will take you closer to your goal, it is time to move the furniture. Put the television in the coldest room in the house where the light is harsh and the seats are hard. Put the things you need to use to take you towards your goal – the computer, the files, the toolbox, whatever it is – in a warm, cosy part of the house where the carpet is thick and the radiators are glowing. You will be far less inclined to watch TV and far more inclined to get on with planning and researching your goal. Added bonus – that's an average of 21 hours a week freed up instantly.

6. Break it down

Having a big goal and nothing else marking the way between here and there can be very daunting. The big goal seems so far away from where you are now that you cannot imagine it ever happening. When you are struggling to make an omelette, the idea of running your own restaurant one day can be impossible to imagine. When you are staring at the wall while waiting for the phone to ring, it can be impossible to imagine that one day your business might employ hundreds of people and be worth millions of pounds.

What's more, if you are purely focusing on your ultimate goal then if you are not careful, you can end up living your life entirely in the future while you wait for your goal to materialize. How many times have you heard friends or work colleagues say they want to do something but are putting it off until they have lost weight, or saved up enough money, or found a partner, or moved house? The problem with thinking like this is you can so easily end up wishing your life away, while waiting for the big stuff to happen.

The solution is to break your goal down into lots of smaller milestones which are near enough to grasp and realistic enough to be achievable. It will focus your mind on what needs to be done right now, and ensure that you don't leave anything out. Which means that you start moving closer to your goal right now too. Which also means you will have less temptation to abandon the whole idea because it is too hard.

7. Monitor your progress

This is an important one. The key point about writing a plan is that it is not just a one-off action, to be scribbled down on a piece of paper and shoved in a drawer and forgotten about. Neither is it set in stone; it is a guide and an aide memoire and can be changed as often as you want. You should update and revise your plan once a year – with a quick read through every six months – to see what you have achieved and to acknowledge how far you have come.

Emma Brockes is a journalist for *The Guardian* newspaper and has interviewed many successful people including Joan Rivers, Alec Baldwin, Nicolas Cage and Susan Sarandon. She has also written two books herself – *What Would Barbra Do?* about her love of musicals, and *She Left Me the Gun*, about her mother's unusual life.

She says: "Successful people are meticulous about documenting their own progress and crossing out when they have done something. I think if you want to get from A to B you have to constantly remind yourself whereabouts you are on that road."

Emma adds: "You have to be very vigilant about the signposts and be absolutely clear in your mind about what you can do in the next two years to take you closer to achieving your ultimate goal. It could be very small things but incrementally they will help you shuffle your way towards your goal. You can't hold in your mind the place where you want to be in several years' time without ruthlessly setting up much more achievable goals in the interim."

Indeed the wonderful thing about having a plan is it gets more and more useful as time goes on. The initial plan enables you to set out your thoughts clearly. But just wait till you get to your second plan, six months or a year later. That's when it really starts to give back, because you begin to see clearly what you have achieved, what has become irrelevant and what is proving to be a major stumbling block. And hopefully, how much closer you are getting to your goal. It is the gift that keeps on giving.

Celebrate your progress too. Give yourself a pat on the back and consciously acknowledge just how far you have come. Throw a party, treat yourself to a pedicure, buy a box set, take your partner out for lunch.

Entrepreneur Lara Morgan is a big believer in making and following a plan. Sixteen years ago she wrote a comprehensive life plan which she now revises every year. Her plan is displayed as an Excel pie chart on her computer and divides the different aspects of her life into eight segments – family, marriage, fitness, learning, business, spiritual, charity and legacy. Every December Lara reviews her progress and sets new targets for the year ahead. To ensure she stays on track, she has a quick look at her plan half way through the year to check where she is up to.

Lara says: "It is a plan that works for me. There is no doubt that it focuses the mind. It is an absolute given that I have achieved more with it than I would have without it. I have a three-point plan for each piece of the pie; it could be taking a child to a special event, or competing in a sporting challenge I have signed up for. It might be that my husband Charlie and I have dinner two times a month. In quiet moments I will look at my plan and think, 'I need to do a bit more of that', and put something in my diary which achieves that goal."

She says that making and sticking to a plan does not have to be a chore: "You don't need to make it a horrible process – it can be extremely joyful when you get to the end of the year and think, I did that. I have got to where I have because I have planned it better and I am more resilient because of it. My life is made up of endless goals, ambitions, targets and intentions because I feel happier when I am working towards something and achieving something."

It clearly works – Lara sold her toiletries business Pacific Direct for £20 million in 2008 and now invests in and advises other growing companies, including Gate8 luggage and Activ-Bod skin care range.

Over to You

1. Make a list of what milestones might be on the way to your goal.

2. Start carrying a small notebook around with you everywhere. Write down thoughts and ideas as they occur to you.

3. How long do you estimate it will take you to achieve your ultimate goal? Put the date in your diary.

"I am always doing that which I cannot do, in order that I may learn how to do it."

Pablo Picasso

4

Supercharge your motivation

"Carpe Diem, seize the day … make your lives extraordinary."
John Keating in Dead Poets Society, *Touchstone Pictures*

Will Greenwood started playing rugby as a child and was in the first team at school. By the time he was 24 he was playing amateur rugby with the London-based Harlequins team at weekends while pursuing a highly paid career as a trader with HSBC bank. So when the English Rugby Union game suddenly turned professional in 1996 Will had a straight choice. To stay on with HSBC and further his career while continuing to play amateur rugby in his spare time – or to find out if he had what it takes to be a professional rugby player. He chose the latter.

Will is very clear about why he made the choice he did. He says: "I took the decision not to be the bloke standing at the end of the bar at the age of 40 or 50 who says, 'Oh I used to play with that lot, I could have played in that team'. I thought, what's the worst that can happen? I just decided to give it a go for two years to see how it went, and I never looked back."

His decision paid off. Will went on to have a professional rugby career lasting ten years. He played professionally for both the Harlequins and the Leicester Tigers and was a member of the England World Cup winning squad in 2003, playing in all but one of England's games and scoring

England's only try against South Africa. He retired in 2006 with 55 England caps and 31 tries to his name and now makes a living as a commentator, public speaker and sports analyst.

It is all very well having ambition but unless you also have the motivation underpinning it then you are never going to achieve your ultimate goal. That's because motivation is the force that turns ambition into action. It is the driver that initiates, directs and maintains the forward motion you need to get you to where you want to be. So the more you can rev it up to the max, the better. Here's how:

Work out why you want to do this

What is driving you to achieve your ambition? What is motivating you to succeed? If you take the time to understand why you are doing this, it will be an incredibly useful tool in actually making it happen. That's because it will help you pinpoint the core factors underpinning your ambition and why they matter so much to you.

The causes of motivation can be complex and over the years many theories have been developed about where it comes from. As far back as 1954, American psychologist Abraham Maslow suggested that people were motivated by solving their unsatisfied needs. To show what he meant, he created a pyramid made up of five levels which showed the hierarchy of needs, from the most basic – food, drink, sleep – to the more complex – self-esteem, recognition and achievement. At the top of the pyramid was self-actualization, the achievement of a person's full potential.

More recently, in the 1990s, Professor Steven Reiss of Ohio State University conducted a survey by questionnaire of more than 60,000 people in Europe, North America and Asia. He concluded that there are 16 basic needs and desires that motivate our actions. These are: acceptance, curiosity, eating, family, honour, idealism, independence, order, physical activity, power, romance, saving, social contact, status, tranquility and vengeance.

Perhaps a simpler way of looking at motivation is to divide it into two forces – those that attract you from ahead and those that drive you from behind. Rather like the power of a strong magnet, both can be really effective at getting you closer to your goal. Let's look at each of these in turn.

1. The factors ahead of you

These are the forces that are urging you on, pulling you forwards. They might include the desire to do any of the following:

- Make something of your life and leave a lasting legacy
- Be an inspiring role model for your children
- Be recognized for your achievements in your field
- Have power or influence
- Be famous
- Be recognized for being good at what you do
- Change the world for the better
- Make a lot of money so you and your family can enjoy a better lifestyle, or so you can take time out from the workplace, or travel, or retire early

- Play a greater role in a team or community
- Do something that will improve the lives of other people
- Have greater control over your life
- Have greater freedom to be creative

2. The factors behind you

These are the forces pushing you from behind, often using your childhood or early experiences to propel you to a better place. They might include a desire to:

- Prove parents or a schoolteacher wrong
- Make up for some failure in the past
- Overcome some perceived deficiency, such as dyslexia, or being short, or having failed the 11-plus exam
- Prove to other people that you can do it, particularly those who doubt you
- Prove that disabilities or early setbacks in life can be overcome
- Achieve more than your parents did
- Achieve more than your siblings have

When brought together, the two kinds of forces can be particularly powerful because they provide a real sense of understanding and purpose to what you are doing. Indeed you may even be able to join them together as the first and second parts of the same sentence, as in:

> I want to be recognized for my achievements because I was always told by my teachers at school that I would never amount to anything.

I want to help children in poor countries receive a better education because I know how much going to school and college has helped me.

I want to be a brilliant doctor because when my father was ill a surgeon saved his life.

It can also be useful to look deeper into your motivation to see what lies beneath it. Why do you want to be an expert in your field? Why do you want to climb that mountain? For fame, money, personal satisfaction, to prove a point, to show that you can? If you can get to the core of what is really driving you, it can help determine the steps you need to take to achieve your goal.

Your goal might be to swim the English Channel. Why? Let's look at what might be motivating you to do this. You will feel a great sense of personal achievement and praise and congratulations from others. You may get your photo in the local paper. You may raise lots of money for charity. You will have something to talk about at parties. But dig a little deeper – what else might your achievement bring? Preparing for the swim will make you much fitter and healthier, and perhaps kick start a new healthier way of living. Doing the swim might give you a better understanding of yourself as a person and of the limits of your endurance. It might prove to your parents that you are capable of achieving something special. It might open the door to more adventures, to meeting interesting people, to writing a book. It might even pave the way to a new job or career – it will certainly stand out on your CV.

Or your goal might be to open a café. Why? To make money, to give yourself a job, perhaps. Maybe even to create a chain of cafés. But now dig a little deeper. The rewards might also be to promote healthy eating, become part of your local community, breathe life into your town, create a place to relax, champion local food producers, provide employment to local people, give you a sense of purpose, enable you to feel that you have achieved something tangible in your life.

Here's a game you can play with friends. Name a successful person and then try to work out what their motivation is for doing what they do and behaving in the way they do. What do you think is the key motivation of Usain Bolt or Judi Dench, or Bill Gates? What factors are driving Anna Wintour, or Piers Morgan or Hillary Clinton? What about Richard Branson, or Marco Pierre White, or Cara Delevingne?

Work out what has been holding you back

Why haven't you achieved your ultimate goal yet? What's stopping you? Factors that might be either consciously or subconsciously be holding you back could include:

- Fear of failure
- Fear of disapproval
- Peer pressure
- Family responsibilities
- Lack of self-confidence
- Lack of self-belief
- Age

- Gender

- Lack of money

- Lack of skills

- Lack of time

- Criticism – or fear of criticism – from family and friends

- Lack of knowledge, or perceived lack of knowledge

Whatever it is, you need to identify it. You can't fight an enemy if you don't know what it looks like. If you can work out what is standing in your way then you can turn your full attention and resources to overcoming it. Even better, once you start to study it in more detail, it may turn out not to be such an insurmountable hurdle after all. If you think the one thing preventing you from achieving your ambition is lack of time, for example, then take a look at Chapter 7 for proven ways to solve the problem.

How to get the most out of your motivation

Your motivation is the single most powerful reason why you will either achieve your ultimate goal or you won't. So you need to make sure it is turned up to the max. Here are seven great ways to squeeze every last ounce of strength out of it:

1. Treat your goal as a challenge

Hugh Facey was running his own fencing business when a Welsh farmer challenged him to come up with a better way of joining wire fences than currently existed. At the time farmers had to go round tying all their fences together by twisting the wires, a process which took a long time and had to be constantly repeated whenever they came loose. Never one to turn down a challenge, Hugh decided to see if he could come up with a solution.

He says: "I was going round seeing people tying fences and I could see there was a problem. I thought there had to be a better way of doing it which would differentiate our fencing from the competition."

In the end he spent four years coming up with a solution – a little gadget, which enabled two wires to be fed through it in the opposite direction and made them both secure and tight. He called it a Gripple. Realizing that it could have many more uses than he had initially envisaged, Hugh sold his fencing business and used the money to start a business to manufacture and sell his wire joiner and tensioner.

It was a good move. From that initial single invention, Hugh's business, also called Gripple, now has a core product range of 2000 items which are protected by 300 patents, employs 500 people and has an annual turnover of £50m. Gripple products, all of which are made in the UK, are used in agricultural fencing, vineyard trellises, for suspending building services such as ductwork and pipework and in seismic and civil construction.

He says: "I like solving problems. I enjoy the satisfaction of finding a solution. That has been my driver all my business life. Our whole business is built on customers saying they have got a problem and then us finding a solution to it."

2. Create a shortcut

Your motivation needs to be easily accessible so you can tap into it whenever you want. And instantly remind yourself why you are doing this. So sum up your motivation in a way that makes it easy for you to remember. Try one of these and see which works for you:

- **Write it down.** Find a phrase that sums up that feeling of excitement you get when motivation strikes. It might be a line from a song or poem, a famous quotation or something you have made up yourself. To get you started you will find a selection of inspiring quotes scattered throughout this book. Once you have found your phrase, repeat it to yourself frequently. You could even stick it up above your computer. It can really help to zap you straight into motivated mode.

- **Visualize it.** You may find that putting up a picture of your ultimate goal helps to focus the mind. Or even putting up a sign. In 2008 a fascinating study conducted by researchers from the New York City Department of Health and Mental Hygiene and published in the *American Journal of Preventive Medicine* found that people were more motivated to use the stairs rather than the lift in a building, simply because they read a sign which said: "Burn Calories, not Electricity". The researchers put the sign up at three sites – a health clinic, an academic building and an affordable housing block – and recorded significantly increased stair use at all sites, both immediately the sign was put up, and even after nine months.

- **Feel it.** This approach works for places too. On a very basic level, if you can associate a feeling with a place then you will remember the feeling each time you visit the place. The next time you visit a department store imagine seeing a display of clothes in the shop window that you designed yourself. Now think about how great you will feel.

- **Listen to it.** Find a piece of music that inspires you and play it whenever you feel your motivation needs a boost. It will instantly remind you how amazing you are going to feel when you achieve your ultimate goal.

3. Find a partner

If you can find a friend or colleague who will set out to achieve a goal alongside you, it can be incredibly motivating. It doesn't have to be the same goal; the important thing is to have someone you can chat to and share notes with. You will inspire and motivate each other, and you will have someone who really understands the sense of achievement you feel when you reach each milestone.

And never underestimate the power of a bit of competition – if you are both trying to reach the same goal, you may both quickly find that you are achieving more than you ever thought possible. That is why children tend to perform better at school when they are placed in groups with others of similar ability. Identifying a competitor, whether they are aware of being your rival or not, can be an incredibly powerful force and drive you forward like nothing else can.

4. Get the right kit

There is nothing more demotivating than trying to make a cake without the right baking equipment, or trying to climb a mountain in old broken down shoes which let the rain in. So do yourself a favour and equip yourself with the appropriate kit for the goal you are trying to achieve. Your motivation levels will thank you for it.

5. Make sure it comes from within

One theory of motivation is that it can be divided into intrinsic and extrinsic motivation. Intrinsic motivation is when we attempt to satisfy a goal we have chosen for ourselves. Extrinsic motivation is when we are driven to do something because of external factors, such as another person's wishes or incentives or rewards offered by someone else. The idea is that intrinsic motivation is far more effective at getting the job done than extrinsic motivation because it comes from deep within you. It is part of you.

There was a wonderful moment in the recent Channel 4 series *Escape to the Wild* that encapsulated this perfectly. The presenter, Kevin McCloud, had just spent nine hours on a sleeper train travelling 400 miles north from a town called Uppsala in Sweden. And then two hours skiing through icy forest, pulling his bags on a sledge behind him, in order to meet Richard and Claire Rees, a couple who left their homes and well-paid jobs in Wales to live in a hut near the Arctic Circle.

Richard and Claire have no running water, and have to haul huge containers of frozen water up from the river each day. They have no electricity or gas and have to rely on wood to keep them warm. They cannot grow vegetables as the ground is permanently frozen so they spend the winter months eating food from cans. There are no roads, the sun doesn't rise for two months of the year and the temperature can sink to minus

40 degrees. But for them, it is clearly paradise. When Kevin asked Richard why they made such an extreme move he just beamed at the camera and said: "Ever since I was a small child, all I wanted to do was live in the forest in a cabin."

6. Don't force it

No one can operate at peak 100% motivation all the time. That doesn't matter. You don't have to feel motivated all the time in order to get closer to your goal. On the days when you are feeling unexcited, tired and hungover, just do the mundane admin tasks that don't require the motivational input. You will still be moving towards your goal. Save the creative stuff for when inspiration strikes.

7. Enjoy the journey

The simplest way to stay motivated is to make sure you enjoy the process as well as the goal. Otherwise you will give up long before the end. There is no point in wanting to be a brilliant architect if you hate the idea of sitting alone sketching for several hours a day. Just as there is no point in wanting to be a top chef if you are not excited about spending most of your time in a kitchen over a hot stove. If you genuinely love the process of what you are doing and not just the end result, that will be all the motivation you need to jump out of bed in the morning and get on with the task.

Love her or loathe her, Katie Hopkins has always been highly motivated to succeed. She joined the army after leaving school with the aim of becoming the UK's first female colonel, but had to leave because she suffered from epilepsy.

Katie then spent 15 years establishing herself as a business consultant before taking part in the television show *The Apprentice,* in which participants compete for a job with entrepreneur Alan Sugar, now Lord Sugar. Her decision not to take up Lord Sugar's offer of a job brought her to the public's attention and she has since determinedly forged a career in the media as an outspoken social commentator, speaking out on controversial issues such as obesity, dementia and immigrants. She is now a columnist for *Mail Online,* has a show on *LBC* radio and her own chat show on a cable channel, and is constantly travelling throughout the country to speak at events and appear on breakfast television. She tweets dozens of times a day on Twitter, where more than 585,000 people follow her.

Katie is clear about what motivates her. She says: "For me it is about leading the conversation and challenging others to be part of that conversation too. I like having the ability to be able to deliver communication so widely. For me it is all about trying to increase my reach."

She adds: "The truth of it is, I genuinely really love working and actually I am rubbish at not working. I would describe myself as driven. I really like the pressure of work, the structure of work, being needed to do things, having my day filled for me. I have always done a thousand and one things – at school it was doing violin and piano to grade 8 when I was 14. I have always felt that innate dissatisfaction with where I am now and where I have got to get to next. I am always looking at what's next, what's next, what's next, almost on a daily basis."

Katie says: "Whatever I have to do to make it work, I will do that. If that involves working 20 hours of the day, or travelling all night to work the next day, or having 24/7 childcare, then that is what I will do."

Having the motivation to pursue your goal sets you apart from all the other people in the world who have big ideas but no drive to achieve them. Understand it, cherish and guard it, because if it disappears it can be very difficult to get back.

Over to You

1. Take a few minutes to write down the factors that are motivating you to succeed.

2. Go for a five-minute run around the block. Or put loud music on and dance round the room and get those endorphins pumping. You will feel ready for anything.

3. Think of the most motivated person you know. What do you think drives them?

"Always bear in mind that your own resolution to succeed is more important than any one thing."

Abraham Lincoln

5

Use the skills you already have

"Promise me you'll remember: you're braver than you believe, and stronger than you seem, and smarter than you think."
Christopher Robin to Winnie-the-Pooh, AA Milne

A few years ago the lady who ran a small annual music festival in the local church at Shoreham in Kent decided it was time to hand over the running to someone else. She asked Sarah Newman if she would take it on. Sarah, who used to work for a law firm and has two young children, had never run a festival before and was initially daunted by the idea. But she discovered she had more skills and experience than she thought.

She says: "It was scary because I hadn't done it before. But I used to be chair of the Parent Teacher Association at my children's school and we organized the summer fete and the Christmas bazaar. I always thought that was just a side part of my life – I did it to be helpful. But it gives you a lot of experience. I didn't really notice I was gaining those skills but through organizing the school events I got experience of laminating things, creating rotas, sending brochures, and deciding who was going to do what and when."

Sarah also discovered, somewhat to her surprise, that she was very good at galvanizing the talents of people around her and finding different ways that they could help, a skill she had learnt while editing a magazine for the law firm she used to work for. She managed to build up a strong team of local volunteers to help her put on the event, including an artist who painted the signs for the festival, and someone who had lots of experience in publicity, websites and finance.

Sarah realized that if the festival was to survive in the longer term it needed to attract a younger, larger audience. So she relocated it from the church to a nearby farm where events could be held in an old barn and surrounding meadows. She also expanded it into an arts and music festival, and chose a line-up of unusual music which she thought would have wide appeal. She says: "I wanted to create a festival I would like to go to."

Her efforts have clearly paid off. Last year her Shoreham Midsummer Festival attracted a record 300 visitors. Highlights included a procession from the village to the farm of people in garlands and costumes, willow sculpting, drumming and a buskers' tent, followed by an aerial circus and barn dance.

The good news is that you too already have many of the skills and knowledge you need to achieve your ambition. In fact, you probably have far more of them than you realize because you have been unknowingly acquiring them and using them in other areas of your life. All you need to do is to identify them, and put them to work. These hidden skills might include:

> **Organizational skills** – gained through work, running a home, planning holidays and family events, volunteering, organizing a party.

Practical skills – gained through DIY, building a garden shed or flat-pack bookshelf, going camping with the kids, repairing a bicycle.

Technology skills – gained through using a computer, using a smartphone, understanding how an XBox or smart TV works, uploading photos from a digital camera.

Physical skills – gained through playing sport, getting fit, dancing.

People skills – gained through negotiating with sales people, querying an electricity bill, buying or renting a house, getting on with the neighbours.

You may be surprised to discover that querying an electricity bill can help you achieve your goal. But so-called soft skills such as negotiating, team building, personal management and communication can play a vital part in turning your ambition into success.

Indeed recent research has found that soft skills can be just as important to personal success as practical skills. A report in 2015 by Development Economics, a consultancy firm, found that developing these soft skills can add up to 15% to an individual's lifetime earnings, and that taken as a whole soft skills are worth £88 billion to the UK economy, a figure which could grow to more than £127 billion by 2025. In the light of the report's finding, a group of businesses and charities, including Mencap, AON and McDonalds, have called for the establishment of a formal framework for school, employers and employees to better promote and recognize soft skills.

Surprise yourself

Roz Savage has made very effective use of all kinds of skills she never knew she had. When she set herself the challenge of rowing solo across the Atlantic Ocean, her only previous experience of rowing was in a boat at university, with seven other people and a cox. But she wanted to see if she could row across an ocean after realizing that she longed for a life of adventure instead of the life she currently had, working in London as a management consultant.

She says: "One day I wrote two versions of my obituary; the one I wanted and the one I was heading for. They were very different. I realized I needed to make some big changes if I was going to look back and be proud of my life."

Roz decided to take part in the Atlantic rowing race, a gruelling race from the Canary Islands to Antigua which is held once every two years. Because she was rowing solo, it would mean having to row for 12 hours a day to cover the 3000 mile journey, and only being able to snatch small amounts of sleep at a time. It was also a huge financial commitment: without any kind of track record or media profile, Roz had to fund £60,000 of the £70,000 it cost to enter the race herself by selling her share of a house she co-owned.

But Roz was determined to achieve her goal so she started training for up to 30 hours a week, doing a combination of running, rowing, cross-training and weight training. She also went on several sailing trips to learn about marine instruments and navigation skills.

For the first two weeks of the race she was seasick and scared, and after only a few days developed tendonitis in her shoulder. Her boat capsized a couple of times and her phone stopped working, cutting off communication with the outside world for 24 days. However unlike some entrants, Roz made it to the other side, arriving in Antigua 103 days later.

The experience made her realize she was capable of far more than she thought. She says: "The best aspect was finding how much I was capable of when I was on my own. I hadn't known for sure before I set out whether I could take care of myself physically and psychologically. And there were many times along the way when I really felt like I had hit my limits. But I really had no choice other than to figure out a way to get through it, and in the process I found I was capable of a lot more than I'd realized."

Indeed two years later Roz went on to row solo across the Pacific Ocean, this time as an independent expedition instead of taking part in a race, doing it in three stages between 2008 and 2010. And the following year she rowed solo across the Indian Ocean, again independently, becoming the first woman ever to row across three oceans. She is now in the *Guinness Book of World Records* and in 2013 was awarded an MBE in the Queen's Birthday Honours.

The experience has profoundly changed her outlook on life, so much so that having started out working for an investment bank, she is now training to be a life coach. Roz says: "Don't waste mental energy asking yourself if you can do something. Just do it. You'll surprise yourself. I did. I am so proud of everything I have achieved. I have shown what an ordinary person can do when they put their heart and mind and soul into it."

Think differently

Sometimes all you need to achieve your goal is the ability to look at it from a different angle.

When Ian Usher's marriage broke down, he was devastated. He and his wife had emigrated from the UK to Australia together and when she left, Ian, then 45, was initially unsure what to do next. But instead of sitting around and moping, he set himself the ambition of creating a completely new life for himself. In a move that generated headlines around the world, he put his old life up for sale on eBay, including his three bedroom house in Perth, Australia, his car, motorbike and parachuting gear, an introduction to his friends and a trial at his job as a sales assistant in a rug shop.

Ian actually ended up selling his house in the more conventional way via a local estate agent. However he used the £83,000 he made from the sale to travel the world for two years, visiting 31 countries as he ticked off a wish list of 100 things he had always wanted to do, including running with bulls, riding an ostrich and learning how to fly a plane. He then wrote a book about his experiences, sold the film rights to Disney, and bought an idyllic island off the coast of Panama for $30,000 (£18,000), where he spent two years clearing the undergrowth and building himself a home. He also found a girlfriend.

When living on a paradise island became too limiting, the two of them set off to travel round the US in a campervan for a year before moving to Shenzhen in China, where they now work as language teachers – at least until their next big adventure shows up. Ian also runs online courses via his website www.ianusher.com.

In the process, Ian has achieved his ambition of creating a new life for himself without any particular skills or qualifications; simply the desire and determination to make it happen.

He says: "When tackling new challenges, chasing new goals and experiencing new adventures – that's when I am at my happiest."

He adds: "Anyone can live a life filled with passion and adventure if they choose to do so. It is simply a matter of deciding what you want to do and then getting on with it. All of life is about choices. The choices you have made in the past have all added up to put you where you are today, to make you the person you are right now. The choices you make today will shape the future you get to live. Make your choices wisely."

Team up with friends

If you really don't feel that you have all the skills you need yourself, one way of getting them is to join forces with other people who also want to achieve the same goal. That way you can pool the skills and experience you have between you.

This is what Scott Carter did. Scott had worked for many years as an oil trader in London and in his spare time brewed beer at home as a hobby. He had always dreamt of turning his hobby into a proper business and starting a brewery, but knew he lacked the skills and money to do it on his own.

He says: "I considered it in the 1990s but I did the maths and couldn't see the economics working. So I dropped the thought and carried on with my real job."

When Scott took early retirement in 2007 at the age of 50, however, he mentioned his ambition of starting a brewery to a group of local business people at a networking event in his home town of Berkhamsted. At the end four of them came up to him and told him that starting a brewery was their ambition too. It got him thinking. Within the space of a few weeks Scott had found eight local businessmen who all wanted to start a brewery. So they did it together.

The benefits of doing it this way have been considerable. First, it has made the project much more affordable. They split the initial £200,000 cost of starting up the brewery between them, putting in £25,000 each. Second, it has given them a wide range of skills and experience to draw on. Between them, the eight founders include a commercial surveyor, a marketing director, an HR director, a sales executive and a logistics manager. They have each taken on different responsibilities at the brewery.

Scott, who is head brewer, says: "This wouldn't have happened without other people doing it too. We split the investment and we split the workload, because it is a fairly labour-intensive industry. You also have to have a huge amount of knowledge – in marketing, HR, health and safety, and technical. Between us there is plenty of knowledge that we can put into the business. It has made it much easier."

Their venture, Haresfoot Brewery, opened in 2014 on an industrial estate in Berkhamsted, the first brewery in the town for 100 years. It now makes 10,000 litres of beer a week, equal to 17,000 pints, and has named its beers after local landmarks. It also stages music events in the brewery and runs guided tours.

Scott adds: "I feel very proud of what we have achieved. There is a fantastic sense of achievement and satisfaction. We have realized what we can do with the skill sets that we have."

The message is clear. You are capable of far more than you think. Try it.

Over to You

1. Write a list of the hidden skills and experience you already have.

2. Now ask your friends and family what they think are your skills and talents. You might be surprised and encouraged by what they come up with.

3. Investigate volunteering opportunities in your area. Would any of these help you brush up your skills while also helping others?

"When you have exhausted all the possibilities, remember this: you haven't."

Thomas Edison

6

Get the other stuff you need

"Big results require big ambitions."
Heraclitus

S teve Backshall was working as a freelance writer for *Rough Guides*, the travel books, when he realized that what he really wanted to do was be a wildlife presenter on television. He had loved adventurous travel and exploration ever since he was a child. But he had no television experience and knew he would need to find a way to show producers that he really had what it takes.

So he bought a cheap home video camera and flew to the most exotic and frightening place he could think of – Colombia. He spent a few weeks in the jungle filming himself with snakes and scorpions, then sent copies of the tape to lots of people in the television industry, along with a proposal for a series entitled "100 things to do before you die".

As Steve says in his book, *Looking for Adventure*: "The way I saw it, my only chance would be to come at it from a different angle from everybody else, and give it every ounce of my tenacity. I was no better than anyone else in the field and I had no experience whatsoever – but I'd want it more, be prepared to sacrifice more, make myself stand out by being a bit different."

His persistence paid off. He was invited to a meeting with the vice president of National Geographic, the television channel, and given a job as their Adventurer in Residence. That led to a job at the BBC, where he worked on several wildlife programmes before becoming the presenter of the hugely popular children's programme, *Deadly 60*.

You too may need to acquire skills and experience to achieve your goal. Fortunately, there are lots of ways to get the training, skills and experience you need, and many do not involve getting on a plane to Columbia. Or cost a lot of money. Let's look at the options:

1. Get the skills and experience you need

Vocational skills training

You don't have to be young to have the opportunity to learn something new. There are courses taking place throughout the country right now that will teach you what you need to know.

A great place to start looking for the training you need is through adult education courses, which are generally held in local colleges. Google "adult education courses" to find your nearest college. These courses may be held in the evening or during the day and can be one-day, part-time or full-time. Some lead to formal recognized qualifications, others do not. Buckinghamshire County Council (www.adultlearningbcc.ac.uk), for example, offers 1279 courses in everything from floristry to basic plumbing. If you are unemployed or low paid you may be able to get assistance with the fees.

There are also many one-off courses available to help you learn a specific skill. If you want to become a winemaker have a look in your local area for a course similar to the Principles of Winemaking course at Plumpton College in Sussex (www.plumpton.ac.uk). If you want to become a writer, see if you can find something like the Arvon Foundation (www.arvon.org) in your area, which offers five-day residential courses at three centres in everything from comedy and radio drama to song writing. If you want to learn how to write computer code you may be able to find a course near you like the one-day course run by Decoded (www.decoded.co.uk).

You may even be able to learn what you need online. Learn Direct (www.learndirect.com) is the UK's largest provider of skills, training and employment services and offers hundreds of online courses from IT to languages. Look for a similar organization in your country.

On the job training

If you are in a job and your ambition lies within the same industry, you may be able to sign up for training courses at work.

Indeed, getting training could be even more useful than you think. A survey by the Open University in 2014 found a complete mismatch between what employees think would get them a promotion, and what employers actually reward. Their survey of 1000 employees and 1000 employers found that while many employees mistakenly believe that working longer hours is one of the best ways to earn a promotion or pay rise, in reality just one in ten employers consider working longer hours to be important. Instead, they are far more likely to reward employees who gain additional work-related qualifications or who go on training courses and are eager to learn new job skills.

Yet despite further qualifications and training being so highly valued by employers, just 11% of workers recognize the value of exploring these – while nearly two-thirds regularly work overtime, with nearly 10% working at least an extra 40 hours per month.

The Open University research found the top three things that people believe will earn them a promotion or pay rise are:

1. Meeting deadlines (37%)

2. Meeting targets (37%)

3. Working longer hours (33%)

However, the top three things employers say will earn someone a promotion or pay rise are:

1. Gaining qualifications, through additional education, which help them become better at their job (46%)

2. Going on work-related training courses (33%)

3. Gaining work-related knowledge through free online courses or by reading relevant books and/or articles (26%)

Working as hard as possible only ranks at number 10. The message is clear, but clearly not getting through – if you want to get ahead, work smarter not harder.

If your company is not very good at sending people on courses, you may need to be a bit proactive. Find the courses you want to go on and explain to your boss why it would benefit the organization if you went on them. You could offer to write a report or make a presentation to the rest of the team afterwards to share what you have learnt. If your organization is not willing to fund it then it may be worth paying for it yourself.

Higher education learning

If you feel a degree will take you where you need to be, you have a couple of options. You can go to a bricks and mortar university as a mature student, either full or part time, or you can sign up to an online degree course such as that offered by Open University (www.open.ac.uk) where you study for a degree at your own pace at home. A mature student is typically anyone over the age of 21 who didn't go to university after school or college.

Taking an MBA has traditionally been seen as a great way of jumping up the career ladder, but it does require a huge amount of time, money and commitment, so do a lot of research first and think hard if it will be worth it. An alternative would be to take a short intensive course at a business school such as Cranfield School of Management (www.som.cranfield.ac.uk), which runs Open Executive Programme courses in areas such as Leadership and Personal Development.

Before signing up for any training or qualifications, do your research properly. Study the prospectus, quiz the organizers thoroughly and if possible ask to speak to people who have already done the course, to make sure it really does do what you are expecting it to do. In particular check it has the right balance between theory and practical hands-on training that you were expecting.

Temporary work

A great way of learning more about the area in which your ultimate goal lies is to get a temporary job in it, no matter how lowly. All kinds of businesses need temporary workers during busy times and over holiday periods. Be prepared to be flexible and say yes to whatever sounds like it might be useful. If you have any kind of typing or computer skills, that will obviously help in getting work in an office, but you can still learn a lot about an organization and an industry by stacking shelves in a warehouse or unpacking boxes and talking to the people working alongside you.

2. Get the money you need

First, work out how much money you will actually require. There are four elements to this so make sure you consider them all:

1. *The amount of money you will need to pay out* – to join a club, buy equipment, attend training courses, hire workspace and so on.

2. *The amount of your current income that you will need to sacrifice in order to pursue your ultimate goal.* You may need to switch to working part time or doing less overtime to free up time to pursue your goal. You may even need to give up your job altogether.

3. *The amount of money you will save by focusing on your ultimate goal instead of doing other things.* Fewer heating bills because you are spending more time out of the house, or less money spent on socializing with friends because you are working on your goal. If you are moving house to pursue your goal, perhaps to be

nearer the sea so you can become a professional surfer, you may find yourself saving a considerable amount of money if rents or house prices are cheaper in the area you are moving to. Or vice versa, of course.

4. *The amount of money that you could choose to save, which you could put towards achieving your ultimate goal.* Buying fewer new clothes, for instance, or switching your weekly grocery shop to a cheaper supermarket, or going on a less expensive holiday – or foregoing it altogether.

Remember that some of these costs and sacrifices will be temporary and others will ultimately reverse themselves, or better. You may need to take a temporary pay cut because you are reducing your current working hours in order to pursue your ultimate goal, but you may end up with a much better paid job.

You may find that the savings you can make in other areas more than cover the costs of achieving your goal. If not, you need to work out what is the shortfall and when you will actually need it – you may require it in stages rather than all at the start. Depending on how much you need, you now have five main options to raise funds:

1. *Borrowing from friends and family.* Make sure both you and they are very clear about whether the money is a gift or a loan. If it is a loan, set out how and when you will pay it back, whether you will pay interest and what happens if you are not able to repay it. You must also ensure that your friends and family can genuinely afford to lend the money to you – parents will often do anything for their children but this is not the time to raid

their pension pots or hard-earned savings if it would make a significant difference to their lifestyle.

2. *Grants and bursaries.* These are most likely to be available for training, education, travel and writing projects. However, they can be hard to find and searching for one relevant to you can be time-consuming. You will also need to be prepared to spend a lot of time filling in forms. And read the small print first – these days grants often come with very specific eligibility criteria. Look online for a directory of grants for your area.

3. *Selling something you own.* If you are lucky enough to own something of value that you no longer need then websites such as eBay (www.ebay.com) and Gumtree (www.gumtree.com) can help you do this.

4. *Personal bank loan, overdraft and credit cards.* Availability will entirely depend on your personal financial circumstances. Likely to cost a lot in interest charges and high risk unless you are confident about being able to repay the amount you owe, plus interest, when required.

5. *Crowdfunding.* A new way of borrowing money that uses the power of the internet to bring together people with projects that need funding with individuals who are happy to invest small sums of money – anything from £10 upwards – to get ventures they like off the ground. Worth investigating, particularly if your ultimate goal is something that others could get excited about.

If you want to raise money for a creative project, the two platforms to check out are Kickstarter (www.kickstarter.com) and Indiegogo (www.indiegogo.com). Both work by enabling individuals to collectively fund projects that they would like to see come to life, whether that be a film festival, video game, technological breakthrough or work of art. People funding projects do not receive any financial reward for their support; instead they may be offered something related to the project. In exchange for funding a project on Kickstarter to create a recipe book about pizza, for example, backers were offered incentives including a signed copy of the book, a T-shirt and a day spent eating pizza with the authors.

If you are seeking to raise money for a business, which could potentially produce financial return for investors, the platforms to use are Crowdcube (www.crowdcube.com) and Seedrs (www.seedrs.com). Investors are given a tiny sliver of equity in the business in return for their funding and hope to make money if the business is sold or starts generating dividends for its shareholders. So far Crowdcube has successfully funded 243 businesses in the UK and elsewhere, with nearly 170,000 people investing £80.7 million between them.

3. Get the equipment you need

If your ambition is physically adventurous, such as leading an expedition to an undiscovered part of the world, you may need some gadgets and services to help you achieve your goal. These might include:

- **Technology.** Depending on what your goal is, you may need a camcorder, smart phone with a camera and a computer with a fast processor and lots of memory. You don't have to get anything flash, but you do need reliable kit that won't seize up the minute you try to use it. If you know nothing about computers or phones, spend a few hours at your local electrical hardware store first and ask a lot of questions. Then get something with a long guarantee and good technical support.

- **Kit.** Tents, survival clothing, vehicles, climbing equipment. You may be able to find what you need for free on a community website such as Freecycle (www.freecycle.org), which has been set up to enable people to recycle unwanted items. You must become a member of your local Freecycle group to take part in the scheme, and you must offer an item yourself first before you can ask for something being given away. Also check out small ad sites such as Gumtree (www.gumtree.com) and Craigslist (www.craigslist.com) for secondhand equipment that people no longer need – you may even find it for free in their "freebie" section.

- **Website.** Depending on the nature of your goal you may need to create a website, for example to enable others to follow your progress. You can create a basic one yourself for free using a website builder site, or pay a few pounds a month if you require more advanced features. Check out website builder sites such as WordPress (www.wordpress.com or www.wordpress.org – they offer different arrangements so check the one the suits you), MoonFruit (www.moonfruit.com), and Wix (www.wix.com). You can buy a domain name from Lowcostnames (www.lcn.com).

- **Communication services.** If your ultimate goal means that you – or your support team – need to be easily accessible at all times, you may need a telephone answering service or virtual PA to answer and deal with your calls. Ideally you need something better than an automated answer machine asking people to leave a message. Check out companies such as Moneypenny (www.moneypenny.co.uk), Avanta (www.avanta.co.uk) and Regus (www.regus.co.uk), all of which offer telephone answering by real people and virtual PA services.

Before you rush out and start waving your credit card around, however, proceed cautiously. You may be able to borrow, lease or try out some of the things you need first to make sure it really is what you need before parting with large amounts of cash. When I wrote my previous book everyone told me I needed a small tablet computer because it would be much easier to carry about than my big old clunky laptop. So I went to a computer store to buy one. Then I spent a day painfully tapping away on its very small keys and peering effortfully into its very small screen, getting more and more annoyed, before finally realizing that I hated it. It didn't work properly either. So I took the tablet back to the shop and got my old heavy laptop out of the cupboard where I had banished it. The next day I happily hauled it to the local café and started afresh.

Think about the choices you make, and make sure they are the right ones for you.

4. Sort out the paperwork you need

Achieving your goal may require visas, permits, licences and consents. If your ultimate goal is to cycle solo around the world, you will need a passport that will be valid for the whole time you are away, and you will need to get the right visas and travel documents for every country you travel though. You will also need insurance both for you and your bike, letters of introduction where needed, and to ensure that you have the right passwords and consents from your bank to be able to access money wherever you are. Before you set off make sure too that your household bills and rent or mortgage will continue to be paid while you are away, that your home and contents insurance will be automatically renewed and that you have written an up-to-date will. You should also consider giving a close relative power of attorney to make decisions on your behalf if you become incapacitated, and getting the relevant paperwork for this.

Over to You

1. Some adult education colleges allow you to try out a class for free. Book one today.

2. Work out how much money you will need to achieve your goal.

3. Take a look at the qualifications you already have. Could they help open a door to where you want to be?

"Any fool can know. The point is to understand."

Albert Einstein

7

Use your time better

"I love deadlines. I love the whooshing noise they make as they fly by."
Douglas Adams

I once bumped into my old college friend David Wolstencroft at the baggage carousel in Los Angeles airport. It turned out we had both just taken the same plane from Heathrow. While waiting for our suitcases we chatted about the flight.

> Me: "Well that was fun. I had some food, drank some wine, watched a couple of films and fell asleep."

> Him: "I proofread a screenplay and wrote the first two chapters of my next book."

David is an award-winning screenwriter, filmmaker and novelist. He created the television show *Spooks*, has written several television drama series including *The Escape Artist* and wrote the feature film *Shooting Dogs*, which starred John Hurt and Hugh Dancy. He lives in a fabulous house in the Hollywood Hills. Now I know why.

It turns out that David has been using his time better for years, even while we were at university. He says: "How do I fit everything in? I prioritize. I read this wonderful article about how Steven Spielberg wanted to make a movie in his last year of high school. So he made his movie at weekends – every weekend – because the pleasure he got from doing that was greater than the pleasure he got from being a regular kid. I took that to heart."

David's time management was learnt from a teacher at school. He says: "I had a geography teacher who told me that 15 minutes is a really useful amount of time. That 15 minutes is not a productive piece of time when it is seen on its own, but it is a component of what you are going to be doing over the medium to long term. If you write two pages of screenplay a week – less than half a page a day – you will have written a feature film by the end of the year."

So while most people tend to just waste their chunks of 15 minutes with faffing about, David uses them to do something productive. Friday night, Sunday morning, after work, before work, whenever. In 15 minutes, he points out, you can write a paragraph – even if it takes the first 5 minutes to get yourself in the right frame of mind. He says: "If I possibly can, I will. It is a muscle. If you don't use your muscle it goes flabby."

David also makes himself take immediate action if he has a good idea, instead of wasting time procrastinating about it.

He says: "I have trained myself to recognize a good thought – I will literally get a twinge in my stomach. Then I will take one specific, concrete real world action. I will make a phone call or send an email, often at night when I'm in LA so that the replies are a bonus when I wake up."

Another person who uses this technique very effectively is Bill Muirhead. The first time I had a meeting with Bill I assumed it would last close to an hour, as most meetings tend to. Bill is one of the founders of M&C Saatchi, the worldwide advertising group, and the Agent-General for the Government of South Australia in Europe, and we had a lot of things to discuss. But when I arrived at his Australia House offices in The Strand, he greeted me warmly before announcing he only had ten minutes to spare before he had to be elsewhere.

There was no point trying to arrange another meeting when I was already there talking to him. So following his lead I dispensed with all the usual polite chitchat and threw myself straight into all the things I needed to discuss, speaking very concisely and noting all the points off on the fingers of my hand as I rattled through them. Bill responded to my queries and suggestions in an equally robust quick-fire way. It was fast, furious and hectic, but after ten minutes we had rather amazingly got through everything we needed to discuss. Job done, and 50 precious minutes of the working day saved.

On the way out his assistant told me that Bill takes all his meetings that way. I left his office invigorated and impressed, and as I made my way across town I realized why Bill is such a successful person. It's because he takes a resource we all have available to us, but he squeezes ten times more out of it, which means that he gets so much more done in a day. It's no accident that he manages to combine two demanding roles.

Here's the thing. Pretty much every successful person is an expert in effective time management. They get a lot more done, a lot faster – and as a result they achieve amazing things. How many times have you heard people say, I'd love to do that – write a book, learn a language, climb a mountain, start a business, whatever – if only I had the time. But the thing is, they do have the time; they just aren't using the time they have got quite as well as they could be.

Here's how to get smarter about using your time:

1. Identify underused pockets of time

Take a look at your average day. What do you actually do in it? If it helps, get a pen and piece of paper and write down what you do every hour. Regardless of what your daily routine is or what your working hours are, there are likely to be pockets of time in your day which you can use to far better effect.

There are 168 hours in a week, which means that even doing a full-time job (40 hours), getting eight hours sleep a night (56 hours) and spending two hours a day travelling to and from work (10 hours) you still have 62 hours a week left over to do with as you wish. So rethink your day to make better use of your time. When novelist Kate Mosse is writing a new book she gets up at 3.30am every morning at her home in Chichester and by 4am is at her desk in her study with a cup of coffee. By the time everyone else gets up – two children, a husband, her mother and mother-in-law – she has already done nearly four hours' work. Kate then spends the day looking after her family, before going back to work at 5pm for a couple of hours.

Her schedule clearly works. Her books have sold millions of copies in more than 40 countries and her best-known book *Labyrinth* has been translated into 37 languages.

2. Play to your strengths

Do you work better in the morning or at night? Are you up at the crack of dawn, raring to go, or are you at your most creative when everyone else has gone to bed? Do you find you have lots more ideas after going for a run? Or while relaxing in a hot bath? Wherever possible, restructure your day around your personal body clock so you are doing the thinking bits when you are most alert and the mundane stuff when you are tired.

If you get it right you will find it exponentially increases your productivity. For someone who is a night owl, an hour in the evening can be as productive as three in the morning. And vice versa. What's more, if you know when inspiration is most likely to strike, you can build in more of the triggers into your day. If going for a swim in the morning always seems to get you thinking about new ideas, try to have one every day.

3. Follow a golden hour policy

If there is a task you keep putting off because you think it will take a lot of time, set aside exactly one hour and commit to work on it without distractions. For optimum effect, choose a time of day when you are at your most alert. Promise yourself that you can stop at the end of the hour regardless of how much or little you have achieved. Now set an alarm so you don't have to continually check your watch, and get to work. No phone calls, no email checking, no getting up to make a cup of tea, nothing else except that specific task.

Fact: you will be amazed at what you can achieve in just one hour. Indeed you may find that by the time the hour is up you have either completed the task, or are so engrossed in it you don't want to stop. This method works for anything from writing a proposal to doing your VAT return to choosing the colours for your website. The secret is to be utterly committed during that golden hour. No distractions, total focus – and the freedom to walk away when the alarm buzzes.

4. Take a two-week view

John Torode is an Australian-born chef and one of the judges on the BBC show *Masterchef*. He has owned two restaurants, *Luxe* and *Smiths of Smithfield*, and written several cookbooks. He also has the perfect antidote to getting overwhelmed. He carries a paper diary with him everywhere and never looks more than two weeks ahead.

He says: "I use a lovely Smythson diary which I have done for the last decade. I order it at the same time every year and I know when it is going to come. My diary has three lovely little bits of silk ribbon in it – one to show this week, one to show next week and one to show the notes at the back. So I know what I am doing for the next two weeks. I used to do it on my computer but there is something very nice about flicking the page of a diary."

When you have a lot to do, it can be easy to get overwhelmed. You tend to look at all the things you need to do and compress them in your brain, so it feels like you have to do all of them immediately, all at the same time.

Happily, there is a straightforward solution to this. Concentrate on what you need to do in the next two weeks, and do not look beyond that. Don't worry about your long-term plan; you have already written that down (see Chapter 3). Your job is to concentrate on what you are doing right now. Looking only two weeks ahead at a time will stop you getting in a panic about how much you have to do. It will help you live more in the moment, and that will help you get more done.

5. Make meetings matter

Meetings can eat up time in an alarming way, particularly if you have to travel far to attend them. So make them count. First, make sure there is a real need for the meeting. Sometimes people suggest meetings because they feel they have to, or even simply as a way of ending a phone conversation or email – let's meet up. If you suspect that is the case, suggest another phone call instead. If you have called the meeting yourself, make sure everyone attending knows what it is for by emailing them an agenda in advance – ideally as a series of questions that need to be answered.

6. Communicate out of hours

Using your time more effectively can actually improve your chances of getting a response from the people you need to contact. Sunday nights are perfect for sending emails because they land at the top of people's inboxes so they see them first when they come into work the following morning. Even better, many people now check their emails on a Sunday evening in preparation for the week ahead, so you may get an instant response.

And I've discovered that 8am in the morning is the ideal time to call or text someone, because it is the magic moment after they have left home and before they reach their office and get swallowed up by their working day. Instead of trying to grab someone between meetings, at 8am they will be on their way to work or at their desk reading the newspapers – in work mode but not yet engulfed in the reality of actually being there. What's more, their PA may not have started work yet so your phone call could get straight through.

7. Relinquish the party organizer role

Are you the one who always ends up being in charge of organizing dinners with friends? Or the one who always arranges family events such as birthdays or holidays? Well, it is time to stop and let someone else have a go. Organizing social events can take up a ridiculous amount of time, tracking everyone down and confirming dates and venues and logistics. So next time you are planning a big get together, don't be the one to put your hand up. And if it always automatically falls to you, ask someone else to do it. Even if they don't do it quite the way you might have done it, it is likely to be good enough. And all that time they are spending trying to book a venue and choose a menu, you can be getting on with achieving your ultimate goal.

And while you are at it:

8. Stop thinking you have to go to everything

You really don't. Yes, it is lovely to be invited, but this doesn't mean you have to go. An evening event is the equivalent of at least four hours you could be spending getting closer to your ultimate goal; longer if you have to factor in travel time and preparation. And even longer if you have to factor in recovery time the next day. If it's a very special event and you are going to have an amazing time, then great, go. But don't go out just because you feel you ought to go. Good friends will understand that there are other things you need to be doing with your time right now. It is just too easy to fritter away valuable time that you will never get back, doing things that you don't really want to be doing. A friend of mine is forever dragging herself out after a long day at work to meet up with casual acquaintances she used to work with, or people she used to spend time with, even though she no longer has anything in common with them, and would much rather spend the evening at home, simply because she finds it so hard to say no.

Avoid falling for the empty diary trick too. If someone invites you to an event, don't make the mistake of accepting simply because it is a long way off and you haven't got much in your diary around that date at the moment. You will still be just as busy then as you are now, you still won't want to go to the event, and you will just have to say no all over again. Imagine the event is taking place this afternoon and make your decision on that basis.

9. Call, don't email

People often email instead of calling someone because it feels much easier and less stressful. But this can mean they are waiting to hear back from someone who might not be the right person. If you talk to someone, however, then even if they are the wrong person, they will usually be able to steer you in the right direction, and might also give you useful information. For example: "You need to talk to John but he's away for two weeks" or "Francine left the company last week. You need to talk to Sue instead." Which you wouldn't have got from an email. Even if they tell you to email someone else, you can now start it with "I spoke to your colleague who suggested that I email you ...", which sounds much better and is more likely to get a response.

10. Now use the time you have saved well

Now that you have freed up all this extra time, make sure you really do put it to good use. The essence of good time management is not just to squeeze more out of every hour, but to actually free up more hours in which to be able to work on your goal. Guard these extra hours you have liberated carefully, and use them wisely.

Over to You

1. Set your morning alarm for 15 minutes earlier than usual. Now see what you can achieve in that time.

2. Set aside specific days or evenings each week in which to work on your goal, and block them out in your diary so you will not be tempted to say yes to anything else.

3. Have a look at your diary for the next two weeks. Is there anything that you could cancel and put the time to better use instead?

"Yesterday is gone. Tomorrow has not yet come. We have only today. Let us begin."

Mother Teresa

8

Focus your energy better

"Action expresses priorities."
Mahatma Gandhi

Deborah Meaden is one of the longest running Dragons on the television show *Dragons' Den*, having been there since the third series. She started her own glass and ceramics importing business at the age of 19 before joining the family business running holiday parks. She went on to take control of the business in a management buyout before selling it for £33 million. She has since invested in many entrepreneurial businesses, from ice cream to photo booths, both through her role on *Dragons' Den* and outside it, and is very involved in advising them and helping them to grow.

Deborah says that much of her success in life has been due to her ability to focus on the things she feels are important. Her school report showed a huge difference between the subjects she liked and those she didn't. She says: "If I wasn't interested in a subject, it would say I was disengaged, disinterested and disruptive. There were lots of 'dis' words in my school report. But if it was a subject I absolutely loved it would say I was focused and engaged. If I am interested in something, you cannot distract me from it. I am like a cat with a mouse. You cannot pull me off it. I think it is one of the characteristics that has helped me."

Deborah's ability to focus intently on one thing at a time is particularly useful now that she has investments in 29 companies. She says: "For each one, when I'm with them nothing else matters. It is like they are my world. When I walk into that room I am just dealing with the stuff that is relevant to that business. That is all I am interested in."

She says that focus is essential to get a project of any kind off the ground: "The only difference between somebody with a business and somebody without a business is that the people with a business say, I'm just going to get on and do it, I'm going to take my first step. If you can focus on something, it is very satisfying and very motivating. It is a great thing to be able to do."

If you are serious about achieving your ultimate goal, you too must channel your energy effectively so you use it for the things that are important. Otherwise it will dissipate into lots of different corners and you will not achieve anything.

Here's how to focus your energy better:

1. Stop multi-tasking

Doing several different tasks at the same time may sound like an incredibly efficient way to get a lot done in a short amount of time. But in reality all that happens is you end up doing everything badly because you are not giving any one task your full attention. The problem is that multi-tasking is a seductive idea because it feels like you are being really clever. It is also quite hard not to do it, particularly if you have loads of stuff to do. Who hasn't tried to write emails to someone while on the phone to someone else? Or surfed the internet while listening to a podcast? Or surreptitiously checked emails while in a meeting? The last one in particular is really tempting, but if you do this you're likely to miss something important that is happening in front of you. And you won't remember the emails you were surreptitiously reading at the time either, because you probably skim-read them and weren't really concentrating. Which means that later you'll realize you forgot to reply to them too.

Sometimes you do have to multi-task. Taking an important call while feeding the children tea is hard to avoid. But mostly you don't have to. So stop. Do one thing well, finish it, then do another thing well. Give each separate task your total attention. Your multi-tasking should begin and end with listening to the radio while cooking or gardening. It takes discipline. But it works.

And while we are on the subject: don't answer your mobile phone if it is not a good time to do so. That is what voicemail is for. You may think you are being efficient but you are actually just being annoying. The most ridiculous response I have had when calling someone is: "I can't talk right now, I'm at a funeral." So why on earth did you answer your phone? Turn it off. If someone really wants to talk to you, they will leave a message and you can call them back when you are able to. That's how phones work.

2. Start writing better to-do lists

To-do lists are a great idea in principle. But only if you keep tight control. If you are not careful your to-do list can end up controlling you, rather than the other way round. That happens when you put so much on it that you can't possibly get it all done. So you give up before you start. Be utterly ruthless about what goes on your to-do list. Three tasks a day are enough. And don't give yourself the option of letting things roll over indefinitely. Three strikes and they are out – you either have to do it or bin it.

And beware of falling into the trap of putting tasks on your list as a way of AVOIDING doing them. Don't write down that you need to phone or email someone if you could easily pick up the phone or email them straightaway. If used like that, your to-do list becomes a procrastination tool – the exact opposite of its real function. Not clever. Make it a rule that if a task will take less than five minutes, you do it right now.

Martin Roberts (www.martinroberts.co.uk) is a property advisor and the presenter of the long-running BBC daytime property auction show *Homes Under the Hammer*. He was formerly a reporter on the ITV travel show *Wish You Were Here*, and the travel editor of *Woman* magazine for 15 years. He is a big fan of to-do lists. He has his written on a piece of paper, which he always keeps to hand.

Martin says: "I am a great believer in lists because I have a thousand ideas a minute which I need to get into some kind of structure. Otherwise there is just too much zipping around in my head."

He explains the appeal: "Lists work in lots of different ways. They assemble your thoughts. They are a memory jogger. And they enable you to see what needs to be done and what you can get rid of. They also give you a sense of satisfaction when you have achieved something and can tick it off."

Martin says that lists are also great for breaking down big projects into smaller milestones. He says: "The most daunting projects can be broken down into smaller chunks. So if you are faced with a massive project, break it down into manageable chunks – then break down those manageable chunks into even more manageable chunks, until you have got these tiny little chunks which are actually really easy and you think you can do two of them today."

One more thing: make your list easy to see. It is too easy to ignore a list that is hidden in the notes section of your phone or in a notebook at the bottom of your bag. Get a sheet of paper and a marker pen. Then either sellotape it to the wall or keep it in your pocket – or both – so you can instantly see what you are supposed to be doing.

3. Get better at making decisions

Perhaps one of the most important things you can do to get closer to your ultimate goal is learn how to make good decisions. If you endlessly procrastinate, or keep changing your mind, you will not only infuriate yourself, you will infuriate those around you and quickly lose their trust and respect.

Gavin Patterson is the chief executive of BT, the telecoms company. He studied chemical engineering at Cambridge University and before joining BT worked for Procter and Gamble and Telewest.

He says: "Making decisions is the single distinguishing characteristic that separates the good from the great. The people that are really outstanding are the ones who are great at making decisions. It is an art more than a science. You don't have to get every decision right; you have to get the majority right. If you can get two thirds of your decisions right, you are doing really well. With the best will in the world you are just not going to get them all right."

Gavin himself used to make decisions in a purely logical, sequential way until he went on a course at his former workplace, Procter and Gamble, which opened his eyes to the idea of making decisions in a more instinctive way.

He says: "Something clicked and I started making decisions in a much more holistic, 360-degree way. My decision-making still has a strong logical basis but now it is also about relying on my gut and trusting my instincts a lot more. The more I have gone through my career, the less decisions are actually black and white. You find you are able to make the case both for something and against something, so it doesn't help to just use logic to make decisions."

Gavin says that knowing when to make a decision can be just as important as knowing what that decision should be: "It is about relying on your gut to say, I am not ready to make this decision, I need to wait. Or I have got to make this decision early because I can sense that if I don't, there is going to be a consequence to it. The timeliness of decision-making is just as important as the effectiveness."

This is how to make good decisions:

- **Make sure you have all the information you need to be able to make a decision.** It can be really hard to make a good decision if you are relying on assumptions or guesswork. Get the facts first. If you can't decide where to live, for example, nail down the information that will influence your decision – how much it costs to rent or buy a property there, how far away it is from the nearest town, how good the transports links are, how much green space there is, how good the schools are, what the average rainfall is. Knowing the facts will significantly reduce your choice, possibly even to just one area. Decision made without you even having to think about it.

- **Find out what your deadline is for making a particular decision.** When do you need to apply for a course, choose a colour, rent an office, get a visa? Whatever it is, find out the date. That way you can prioritize the decisions you need to make, and make the crucial ones now while leaving the others for later. It may even be that making the most urgent decisions now simplifies the decision-making for the other ones, because it reduces the choices available to you.

- **Put your thinking down on paper.** It doesn't have to be neat; doodles and diagrams are fine. Just get it down. You will get a much clearer idea of the big picture if it is in front of you in black and white, not just inside your head. Plus you can refer back to it later.

- **Ensure that you are making your own decision and not the decision that someone else wants you to make.** If you feel under pressure to make a particular choice, or even to make a choice at all, pause and reflect. And beware the "assumed choice" tactic. The simplest way to get someone to agree to something is to get them to make a decision beyond the one they should be making – asking them to choose between two types of pizza when you haven't even given them the choice of whether they want

Italian or Chinese food. Make sure you are making the decision that needs to be made.

- **Understand the risks of choosing each possible option – and the risks of not choosing it.** You can't avoid risk entirely, but you do need to ensure you are only taking risks you can live with.

- **Listen to your gut.** In some situations tapping into your unguarded emotional response can be extremely useful, particularly when there is no automatic "right" or "wrong" decision. When choosing a home to rent or buy you may get a strong sense of whether or not you'd like to live there within seconds of setting foot in the door. However, you still need to subject it to the same objective analysis as the other possible options to ensure that it really is the right decision. I once fell in love with a studio flat where the bed was basically a mattress in a large cupboard. It seemed like a fun place to live until I realized that I wouldn't even be able to sit up in bed and read a book, and would absolutely hate it.

- **Sleep on it.** Your brain will continue to mull over the decision to be made even when you are not consciously thinking about it, so if possible give it time to whirr away while you are asleep. It may give you useful insights. When you wake up the next morning you are likely to be much clearer about whether you are making the right decision.

- **Finally – never put off making decisions that need making.** As soon as you have enough information to make a sensible, informed decision, do it and move on to the next one. Even a poor decision is usually better than no decision at all because at least it gives you something to work with.

As Martin Roberts says: "If you don't make a decision, it hampers your chances of success. So just make the bloody decision. Because even if you make bad decisions, you learn from them. And if you make good decisions, you will have made them quickly so can benefit from that."

4. Stay healthy

Simon Cowell does 500 push ups before starting work and has three baths a day. Singer Taylor Swift runs on a treadmill before every show and takes raspberry and walnut salad dressing with her everywhere. Barack Obama starts each day with a cardio and weights session in the gym.

The best way to keep your energy levels high is to look after yourself properly. It makes a lot of sense. Happy body equals happy mind – equals your best chance of achieving your ultimate goal.

The perfect healthy regime to help you move closer to achieving your ultimate goal has four essential ingredients:

1. **Eat right.** Consuming the right kind of food can make an enormous difference to how you feel, the level of energy you have, and therefore how well you perform. Which means healthy food is in, and junk food is out. Go easy on the carbs too.

   Lucas Hollweg is a food writer and author of the cookbook *Good Things to Eat*. He says: "What you eat and when you eat it can make an enormous difference to your energy and motivation. Eating too many carbs is likely to make you want to curl up in the corner and go to sleep rather than going out there full of ideas. Eat a bit of protein, lots of green vegetables, not too much starch – those are the things that keep you feeling alive and alert."

It is also important to make time for proper food breaks rather than simply eating on the go, says Lucas: "Food should be a source of happiness rather than simply a source of fuel. It puts you in a much better place to go out and do something positive. You are more likely to succeed when you are feeling happy than when you are feeling stressed. That doesn't mean sitting down to a three-course meal. Even stopping for a few minutes to savour a ripe peach can be blissfully uplifting. A moment of quiet reflection with something delicious is a really good starting point for conquering the world."

2. **Get enough sleep.** That means get enough for you, not former British Prime Minister Margaret Thatcher who famously survived on four hours' sleep a night. It can be hard to think straight when you are sleep-deprived, let alone make sensible decisions or get anything done.

A survey by Professor Richard Wiseman of the University of Hertfordshire found that getting enough sleep could play a significant role in achieving goals. When he asked 1000 people to rate the quality of their sleep and how successful they were at achieving their New Year's resolutions, Professor Wiseman discovered that 60% of the people who said they slept well achieved their resolutions, compared to 44% of those who slept poorly.

Only you know how much sleep you need. There is no "one size fits all" and everyone is different. But health experts say that in general adults need between seven and eight hours a night. You should also take these two steps to ensure it is good quality sleep: a) stop using computers and other electronic devices an hour before bed otherwise you will find it hard to switch off. And b) don't use your smart phone as an alarm clock, because if it is by your bed you will be tempted to check your emails and see what's trending on Twitter through the night.

3. **Take plenty of exercise.** Studies show there is a proven link between exercise and energy. Which means you can significantly increase your productivity and performance, and the chance of successfully hitting your ultimate goal, by getting your running shoes on. Indeed, research suggests that the more fit you are, the more resilient your brain becomes and the better it functions both cognitively and psychologically. So go for a walk or jog every day, or run or swim a few times a week.

4. **Build in down time.** Work hard – then switch off and immerse yourself in something else for a while. Ideally something which uses a different part of you. If you have been staring at a computer, bake a cake or do some gardening. If you have been building something with your hands, read a book or listen to music. Don't embark on something so complicated and involved it will end up taking days – now is not the time to start repainting the kitchen – but just something light and fairly non-taxing that will give the other bit of your brain a rest.

5. Just say no

One of the most powerful tools in life is learning how to say no to things. It can be hard to say no because it somehow feels wrong. But if you are going to achieve your ultimate goal rather than just talking about it, there will be times when you need to turn down suggestions and opportunities, no matter how exciting and lovely, because they don't take you nearer to where you want to be. It's like a neighbour spotting you walking along the road and pulling over to offer you a lift in the opposite direction. Very kind, but not actually very helpful.

Here are tried and tested strategies to help you say no:

- Don't always feel you have to give a detailed explanation about why you are saying no. One line will suffice. Perhaps the most useful five words ever invented are "Not one for me, thanks." Genius.

- If it is a no, make it absolutely clear that is what you are saying and that there is no room for doubt. Don't try to soften the blow by offering hope when there is none. You will simply end up wasting both the other person's time, and yours. Because if they think there is a glimmer of hope that you will change your mind then they may get in touch again with further suggestions.

- Don't be mean. An increasingly common way of avoiding saying no is not to respond at all, in the hope that something else will come up and the other party will have to say no first, thereby saving you the pain of saying no yourself. But we all know there is nothing more infuriating than not getting a reply when you have contacted someone, so don't inflict that pain on others. Whether you send an email or say it in person, do it and do it quickly. A fast no is always preferable to a slow nothing.

- Don't feel bad about it. You don't want to upset people and you want people to like you. But saying no to someone frees them up to find a yes elsewhere, which may be more appropriate and fulfilling for them than your yes would have been anyway.

- Suggest someone else. If you think it might be helpful, suggest the name of someone else who would be a good alternative in your place. But don't use this as a cop out – the suggestion must be genuinely useful.

- Practise saying no. It really does get easier you more you do it. Say it now. NO. NO.

Stephen Carlile is a professional stage actor whose roles have included Scar in the UK touring production of *The Lion King*. He now plays Captain Hook in the US touring production of *Peter Pan*. He has gradually learnt to have the courage to turn down things that won't take him to where he wants to be.

He says: "A few years ago I started to say no to things that I didn't really want to do, because I wanted to see what would happen if I just held back and waited for something good. So I waited for about seven months and something brilliant came along. Then when that project came to an end I did the same thing again. I was offered a couple of parts but I thought that if I said yes to them, something better might come along which I wouldn't be able to do. And because I waited, I was asked to go to America to be in *Peter Pan*. It is a brilliant production and was worth waiting for. You have to stay focused on your goal otherwise it won't happen."

Over to You

1. Arrange your bedroom for the best possible night's sleep. Unplug gadgets from by your bed, get an alarm clock so you can turn your phone off, check that your curtains block out the light, buy a supportive pillow.

2. Keep a food diary for a couple of days and note the times when you are most lacking in energy. Consider how you could make simple tweaks to your diet to improve your concentration levels.

3. Make sure you are registered with a doctor, book a dental check-up and eye test, and deal with any health concerns you may have.

"Things which matter most must never be at the mercy of things which matter least."

Johann Wolfgang von Goethe

9

Do your research

"The more that you read, the more things you will know. The more that you learn, the more places you'll go."
Dr Seuss

There used to be a sign pinned to the wall in the business section of *The Sunday Times* newsroom. It read: "Assumption is the mother of all f**k ups." It was a reminder to journalists and sub-editors working on the section to check every fact before allowing it to go in the paper. Dates, place names, titles, everything had to be checked and no-one should ever assume something was true just because it sounded like it might be.

That sign should be pinned to everyone's wall. One of the reasons why projects fail is because people didn't do their research properly. They didn't check how big the market for bespoke treehouses really is; they underestimated how long something would take to do; they didn't realize they would need a permit; they didn't check if they would be able to get a bank loan.

That's sad, but even sadder is when people don't even attempt to pursue their ambitions because they let a false assumption stand in their way. Too many people consciously or subconsciously stop themselves from doing exciting and brilliant things because they assume things work in a certain way, or because they think they are not allowed to do something, without doing any further checking. Yet they could be completely wrong.

When I was applying for a place at university I knew of several people my age who deliberately chose not to apply to Oxford or Cambridge universities. Not because they weren't clever enough, but because they assumed they would feel out of place and that those universities were not places for people like them. They were entitled to their own opinion of course, but what I found really hard to understand was that they had come to this conclusion without actually doing any research of their own to find out if it was true. Instead they were basing their knowledge and decision entirely on the outdated impression they had of Oxford and Cambridge universities, which they had picked up from hearsay, media stereotypes and Merchant Ivory films. It may be that having done some research they would still have concluded they did not want to go, but basing such an important decision on ignorance seemed then, and still seems now, a really poor idea.

The fact is, knowledge is power. If you ever get stuck in a lift with a really successful person and are searching for a topic of conversation which will see you through until you are rescued, ask them to explain how their industry works. You are likely to discover that they know their industry inside out, back to front and upside down. They will know who the important people are, where the power lies, how decisions are made, and who really makes them. Successful people leave nothing to chance and neither should you.

The good news is there is nothing to stop you getting the knowledge you need about how your chosen area of interest works. Regardless of what area you are going into, there are likely to be six key things you need to find out:

1. Understand how your chosen field or industry works

One of the key ways to turn ambition into success is to completely immerse yourself in the world in which you want to progress, so you are able to identify and act on the opportunities which will help you move ahead. That means finding out what makes it tick. You need to know which are the different groups who operate within it, who supplies what to whom and why, how and when they do that, and how they get rewarded or paid for it. You also need to work out the human dynamics – why do people in the industry behave in a certain way, what are they trying to do and what is driving them?

Take the book publishing industry as an example. If your ultimate goal is to be a best-selling author, it can be extremely useful to understand how the relationship between authors, literary agents and publishers works and to understand what motivates each of these different groups and how they get paid. It can also be useful to understand where the power within the industry lies, or how decisions are made about what books get published. And crucially, how the balance of power is changing with the emergence of self-publishing, e-books and so on. If you really and truly want to be that bestselling author, you need to make it your job to understand all of this.

As Deborah Meaden, one of the Dragons on *Dragons' Den*, points out, you don't have to be an expert, but you do need to know enough to be able to ask the right questions. When she ran her family's holiday parks business she learned how to change a gas bottle, how to pull a pint and how to move a caravan, because it was important to her to understand how these things worked. She says: "I am an expert in absolutely nothing. I am a generalist. A lot of successful people are generalists. Generalists know what they have got to know, so they know what they don't know and what they need to ask. So many people blindly go through things and don't realize they have missed the great big white elephant in the room, because they didn't know enough to know that it was there."

2. Find out who the key players are

These might be companies, organizations or individuals. Check out their websites, sign up to their newsletters, read their blogs, visit their premises, become a customer. Study review and comparison websites to find out what people really think of them.

Read any profiles and interviews of the key players that you can find in the media and check out any books they may have written. Keep a look out for any opportunities to hear them speak, at a networking event or conference or via a podcast or webinar. Every industry has a calendar of events which all the key people attend: annual dinners, awards ceremonies, national conferences, trade shows, depending on what kind of industry it is. Find out when they take place, who is speaking at them and whether the public can attend too.

Remember too though that power structures do not last forever and even the biggest organizations can have ambitious disruptive newcomers nibbling at their toes. Try to identify them, too.

Careers advice services can be an invaluable source of information about specific companies and industries. If you were at college or university, as a graduate you may still be able to make use of their careers advice service no matter how long ago you left. You may even be able to find contact details of other graduates already working within the industry you wish to enter.

Also investigate open days, taster sessions and open access training opportunities within a particular industry. Some industries are better at this than others but it can be an amazing way of gaining insight. Diamond Light Source, for example, is the UK's only synchrotron, a particle accelerator which creates x-rays and is one of the most advanced scientific facilities in the world. It regularly holds free open days for the public at its facility at Harwell in Oxfordshire. The open day includes demonstrations, talks, activities and a tour of the synchrotron, which produces a light 10 billion times brighter than the sun.

3. Find out what the issues are

What are the big challenges facing your chosen field, what implications do they have for what you want to do, and how might they represent an opportunity or a threat to your ultimate goal? You really wouldn't have wanted to go into the mangle producing business just before washing machines were invented, and neither would it be a great idea to arrange a wine-tasting festival for January when many people give up drinking alcohol for a month.

The simplest way to find out the issues is to get reading. Read the trade press for your chosen area or industry and sign up to any relevant websites and online newsletters to get the latest news and insight. If your ambition involves boats, trade magazines include *Boat International, Waterways World, Boat Trader, Practical Boat Owner, Sailing Today, Yachting World, Yachts and Yachting.*

If you don't know which publications cover your chosen field there is likely to be a database that can provide the information you need. In the UK, look in the latest edition of the *Writers' and Artists' Yearbook* which lists all UK magazines and journals. Or check out WHSmith's website (www.whsmith.co.uk) which lists nearly 2500 magazines on every conceivable topic.

4. Find out where you might fit in

Big goals are much easier to achieve if you can put yourself in a supportive environment. If you can find people that understand what you are trying to do, you are already halfway there.

If your goal is career-oriented, find a company to work for which actively encourages and supports ambition. This can make a huge difference to your chances of success. Make sure it is a fast-growing company too – that way you won't have to wait long for a position higher up in the organization to become vacant in order to progress, because new roles will be created all the time. Look out for annual comparison lists – in the UK, *The Sunday Times* annual *100 Best Companies to Work For* list is a good place to start, while in the US, *Fortune Magazine* produces an annual list of *100 Best Companies to Work For*. Randstad, a global recruitment firm, produces lists of the best companies to work for in many countries throughout the world. In each case firms are typically judged on the extent to which employees feel they are stretched and challenged by their job, as well as how happy they are with their pay and benefits.

In 2015, according to *The Sunday Times* list the ten best companies to work for with a workforce of between 250 and 3500 people were:

1. Simply Business – online insurance firm

2. Red Carnation Hotel Collection – hotels

3. Chess – telecoms reseller

4. Moneypenny – telephone answering service

5. Holiday Extras – travel support services

6. Connect Catering – contract catering

7. Mishcon de Reya – legal firm

8. Zenith – commercial vehicles provider

9. Childbase Partnership – children's nurseries

10. Vacherin – contract catering

Jason Stockwood, the chief executive of Simply Business, which took the number one slot, says: "We definitely encourage ambition. If we can help people fulfil their potential while they are working, that usually drives their performance and their desire to help the business and its strategic goals as well. In a growth company you need people who have drive and ambition beyond the job you are recruiting them for. You want to feel like they are bringing something to the party that isn't there already."

Indeed, Simply Business has now created a by invitation only development programme for its most ambitious employees. They meet once a month to solve real live challenges facing the business. It is a great way for those with ambition to stand out from the crowd – and also a great way for Jason and his team to spot those with the qualities to join the management team in the future.

Jason says: "I look for three things to identify ambitious people – people who excel at the specific thing you hire them to do, people who really want to take things on individually and drive them beyond what you specifically ask them to do, and people who really give above and beyond what is expected from them. Ambitious people are motivated beyond their specific role and current capabilities to do more than they are currently hired for."

If your goal is lifestyle-oriented, take the time to find out where the like-minded people are. I'm fascinated right now by the whole concept of digital nomads, that adventurous group of people who travel the world with a smartphone in one hand and a laptop in the other. Digital nomads differ from other long-term travellers in that they use the capabilities of the internet to enable them to work remotely while they travel, often accomplishing as much as they would working in an office in their home country. In theory this means they can keep going indefinitely if they choose, and even develop their careers at the same time. Digital nomads need four key things for the perfect location – good mobile phone and wi-fi connections, inexpensive accommodation and living costs, a good level of personal safety and a vibrant community of like-minded souls (and, arguably, lots of sun and a beach, otherwise what's the point – you might as well have stayed at home).

There are several websites that can tell you the perfect places in the world to be a digital nomad. Nomad List (www.nomadlist.com) rates places according to seven key factors, and has put Budapest, Bangkok and Taghazout in Morocco as its top three. DIY Genius (www.diygenius.com) puts Koh Pha Ngan in Thailand, The Oaxacan Coast in Mexico and Lake Atitlán in Guatemala as its top three destinations.

5. Keep asking questions ...

Round about the age of four, children start asking questions. Dozens of questions a day, one after another, often without pausing for breath. And they basically don't stop till they turn eight. Not simple questions either. Why doesn't the sun fall out of the sky? What are flowers made of? Why was I born second? Why can't animals talk? On and on until your head feels like it is about to explode.

And watch how they play. They are forever trying things out, testing them, dropping them on the floor to see what will happen. If you haven't been to a museum for a while, pay a visit – almost everything is interactive now so children can find out about things in a very hands-on way. At the Natural History Museum there are boxes to put your hands in and guess what is inside; at the Science Museum there are water features to get wet in and buttons to press and levers to turn and things to climb on and in.

If that sounds like fun, good. You too need to tap into your inner child and rediscover your natural curiosity, because that is the way you will find out everything you need to know.

Michael Acton Smith is the founder of entertainment company Mind Candy and the creator of Moshi Monsters, which began life as a drawing, grew to become a website with over 80 million registered users and has now expanded into books, toys, magazines, trading cards, music, apps and a movie. Mind Candy now employs 100 people and has a turnover of many millions of pounds.

Michael says: "Being very curious is important. I think that is a very good trait to combine with ambition because whenever I am starting a new venture I just dive in and splash around as much as I can, going to relevant conferences, drinking coffees with anyone I can, reading any relevant books."

He adds: "I have always had a voice that whirrs away in the back of my mind, spurring me on to try to do new things. I love creating stuff and dreaming up new ideas. I am always wanting to be doing new things and getting into new situations. I like stuff that makes you a bit scared and fearful when you talk about doing them. When we undertook the Moshi journey it started as just a little sketch on a piece of paper. But I always wanted to build it into this huge entertainment company with lots of different products in lots of different countries that would have an impact on millions of people."

Remember that no research is ever wasted, even if it might not be obvious at the time what use it is. As novelist Kate Greville writes in the introduction to her book, *The Idea of Perfection*, which won the Orange Prize for Fiction in 2001,

"I did a great deal of research, and even though not much of it appears directly in the book now, the writing would not have been possible without it."

6. ... but know when to stop

Beware of using research as an excuse to delay taking action. You can't ever hope to know everything you need to know. So at some point you have to decide you have enough to get going, and get on with it.

As Deborah Meaden says: "Asking questions can be a very clever way of delaying the moment where you have actually got to make a decision. Market research is a fantastic thing, but if you are still doing it three years later you have probably missed your moment."

Over to You

1. Write down three questions that you would really like to know the answers to in order to achieve your goal.

2. Now identify the person or people within your chosen area who are most likely to know the answers.

3. Think about how you might be able to contact them and ask your questions.

"Chance favours the prepared mind."

Louis Pasteur

10

Get out there and make it happen

"Believe you can and you're halfway there."
Theodore Roosevelt

I always love the bit in James Bond films where Q briefs him on all the gadgets he is going to use in his mission: the exploding pen, the watch fitted with a laser beam cutter, the ring containing a miniature camera. Then Q hands him the briefcase and wishes him luck as James Bond says goodbye to Miss Moneypenny and heads out to deal with the baddies and make everything right again.

The good news is that you too have reached the really exciting bit of your mission to achieve your ultimate goal. You've made a plan, done your research and fine-tuned your skills. Now it's time to put it all into action. Remember when you were finally allowed to use a power drill after years of only being allowed to watch from a distance as a parent used it? Or when you were finally old enough to get behind the wheel of a car after years of being confined to the back seat? Well it's like that, only better.

Here's how to do it right:

1. Look for opportunities

When Kate Jenkins started making brownies in the kitchen of her cottage in the Gower Peninsula, in Wales, she sold them in the local village shop. Eight years on, however, her venture has become a fast-growing business with a turnover of £300,000. Kate typically makes and sells 40–50 boxes of brownies a day, except when she appears on QVC, the shopping channel, when she can sell 1000 boxes in six minutes.

The former family kitchen has been extended and turned into a commercial kitchen, while a "brownerie" housing an office and packaging area has been built in the garden. Her husband has given up his job to work in the business full time, along with two assistants who do the cutting and packaging.

Much of the success of the business has been due to Kate's ability to spot opportunities – and being fearless enough to act on them. When she heard that the television series *Torchwood* was being filmed nearby Kate immediately sent five boxes of brownies down to the set. Half an hour later the lead actor John Barrowman was on the phone, telling Kate that her brownies were fantastic, and asking where he could buy them. Kate says: "He has been my customer ever since. He sent them to the whole cast."

Another time an eagle-eyed customer spotted a tweet from Emma Freud, Richard Curtis's partner, asking how she could get hold of a large quantity of delicious cakes or scones to cheer up a film crew while they were making the movie *About Time* in a remote part of Cornwall because the weather was awful. The customer suggested that Emma get in touch with Kate, who immediately offered to courier down a huge box of brownies to the film set the next day for a nominal charge.

Emma Freud was delighted and has since become a huge supporter – and customer – of Kate's brownies. She orders them for parties, sends them as thank you presents to friends, and buys them for her son's birthday each year. She even invited Kate to the film premiere of *About Time* in London. Kate says: "She knows she can trust me and that I am not just trying to make a quick buck, because that is never what it is about."

Indeed Emma even recommended Kate and her brownies to the *Henley Literary Festival* when she took part in an event there. So now Kate supplies her brownies backstage at the festival every year and presents all the authors taking part with a box to take home.

Kate says: "I never pay for advertising; I use my brownies as marketing instead. And that is where you have got to see the opportunity, because if you get them in the hands of the right people, they will tell other people about them. For me it is not about selling one or ten or a hundred brownies as a one-off – I want people to get interested in my brownies and to keep coming back. My customer loyalty is quite unbelievable."

John Torode is also a big believer in seizing opportunities. Indeed that is how he ended up on television, as presenter of the cookery show *MasterChef*. In 1995 John was running his restaurant *Smiths of Smithfield*, when the producers of the breakfast television show *This Morning* got in touch to ask if they could film him cooking as part of a short segment on how restaurants were changing the face of Britain. John agreed and enjoyed it so much that afterwards he spoke to the woman who had organized the filming: "I said, I loved doing that, it was great. If you ever want somebody to do some cooking with you guys on your programme, I would love to come and do it. She looked at me and said are you serious? The next thing I knew, I was heading off to Liverpool and cooking on the Richard and Judy show. And that started it all."

John says he has learnt a lot from his father: "My father has many sayings and I use quite a lot of them. One is that you have got to blow your own trumpet otherwise someone will use it as a spittoon. You have got to go out there and say, 'G'day mate, how are you, I'm John.' You have got to have a bit of bravado."

He adds: "Nothing comes to you. I don't just sit on the sofa and cross my fingers and close my eyes and hope something happens. I search for things. Luck comes to those who make their own luck. You can win the lottery but the first thing you have got to do is enter it. The world is an extraordinary place and there are plenty of opportunities out there. I know I will never get to do them all but I would like to do a lot of them."

You also need to spot opportunities in the workplace if you want to get to the top. These days there are far fewer structured career routes, even within professions, which means if you want to get ahead you will have to create and manage your own career path. And most likely not just within one organization, but several of them.

Start by looking at the bigger picture – what roles are likely to be needed in your organization in the near future? What positions are likely to be expanded, or become more senior, as the needs of the organization change? A couple of years ago, for example, dealing with a firm's social media might have been a relatively junior role. However, as the importance of social media to an organization has increased, so has the responsibility and seniority of the role. Technology too is enjoying a surge of importance. Once primarily a functional role, a growing number of firms are now including chief technology officers on their management boards.

Look also at what characteristics are being increasingly valued within your organization. Is having a certain qualification the key to moving ahead? If so, it might be worth seeking out a way to acquire it. Or is breadth of experience a prized commodity? If so, it may be worth taking a sideways move to gain more wide-ranging experience, in order to position yourself for an upward move later.

Indeed sometimes it might be worth going away and then coming back. Particularly if you find it hard to move ahead in the company you work for because you have been pigeon-holed into a certain kind of job, or level of status. If people are so used to thinking of you as working in the post room that they find it hard to imagine you doing anything else, you are in trouble.

Happily there is a solution to this. Other companies, even in the same industry, will have a far less rigid expectation of what you can do and what limits they should place on you, simply because they have never seen you coming to work and heading for the post room each day. So they may be more inclined to let you shine and move ahead. Once you have got to the level you feel you should be at, you can always move back to your old company, if that is where you want to be.

This is exactly what happened to Emma Roadnight. She started out as an advertising assistant on the classified section at *Top Santé*, a monthly health and beauty magazine. But after a couple of years she had a chat with her boss and realized she would have to leave if she was to further her career within the industry.

She says: "I had conversation after conversation with the management at *Top Santé* about how I wanted to see my career going, but they wanted me to stay as an advertising assistant because I was doing such a good job. They would quite happily have pigeon holed me there all the time, rather than giving me options to progress up the ladder or try something different. So I had to move companies to get to the next step. I would never have got the roles I did if I had stayed there."

So Emma got a better job as a display executive on another magazine and by moving magazines each time she wanted to be promoted, after seven years she ended up returning to *Top Santé* as its commercial director, in charge of its entire revenue stream. It was a promotion she would never have achieved if she had stayed at the magazine.

She says: "When I came back it felt like it was meant to be, because I knew the magazine so well and had worked on it when it was first launched in the UK. It was a real sense of achievement. All the management had changed as well while I had been away so I could really take control."

2. Sow seeds

It can be hard to know which actions you take are going to lead somewhere meaningful and which are not. So stop trying to second guess the universe and instead do lots of actions to increase the chance that some may take root and work out. Don't send one email to one person; send 10 emails to ten people. Don't just attend one networking event; go to six. All of these activities may be small in themselves but the more seeds you sow, the greater chance that some of them will lead to something greater. It takes away the guesswork of trying to decide which action you take is going to matter, and it takes away the pressure on any one single action succeeding. It also stops you sitting around waiting for that crucial email or phone call to land.

Have realistic expectations too. Don't get outraged or upset if you don't get a response. People are busy, life is busy, and if an email or phone message doesn't immediately strike a chord, they may well leave it instead of taking the time to reply. They are not being rude, they are just being efficient with their time, and it is important to respect that. Yes, it is maddening and infuriating, but you have to let it go. Instead manage your expectations so that getting a response of any kind becomes a huge achievement.

Here's a tip – if you don't receive a reply, simply resend the email a week later, as a fresh email, and see what happens. It may be that they simply didn't see your email the first time but do spot it now, and you may get a reply. But don't simply forward the original email with the words "Just checking you have seen this?" at the top. For some reason this makes me furious, because it comes with a veneer of solicitous enquiry combined with an undercurrent of suppressed outrage and pained disappointment. I may be the only one who feels this way. But I suspect not.

Do make sure though that it really is a week later when you send your fresh email. Time moves at a different speed when you are the one trying to get a response, so give the other person the opportunity to consider, digest and possibly respond first. Resending your email after two days is not acceptable and will just make them cross.

If you do get a response to anything, always reply back, even if someone is saying no to you. Don't do this in order to harangue them or beg them to change their mind, but simply to say that's fine, thank you for getting back to me. Politeness and charm go a long way in this world and if your paths do cross again, the other person may search out your email, see your dignified response and feel much warmer towards you.

One more thing. If you want someone important to notice you, send them a letter. By special delivery or by courier, personally addressed to them, so they have to sign for it. Expensive, but worth it. No-one sends letters these days so natural curiosity alone is likely to make them open it and read it.

3. Join the conversation

People cannot mind read. If you are trying to do something which requires their interest and involvement, they won't know about it unless you tell them. This is true whether they are a potential customer, a possible investor, your boss, a senior person in your field, or the world at large. If you want people to listen, start talking. Here's how:

- If your goal is to be appointed a senior director in charge of a division, arrange a meeting with your ultimate boss and set out what you want to achieve and how you plan to go about achieving it. Remember, it is not up to the organization to understand your aspirations and ambitions and provide the route. You have to make it happen yourself.

- If your goal is to get the world to notice you, get onto social media. Depending on who you are trying to reach, sign up to Twitter (www.twitter.com), Facebook (www.facebook.com), LinkedIn (www.linkedin.com) and, if relevant, create your own YouTube (www.youtube.com) channel. Instagram (www.instagram.com), Vine (www.vine.com) and Pinterest (www.pinterest.com) might be useful too.

- If your goal is to share your thoughts and ideas, write a blog. My sister Sarah is a financial journalist and spends a lot of time at business lunches, which are often held in smart restaurants and hotels such as the Savoy, Claridges or the Ivy. While the lunches are a chance to talk to business executives and find out more about their companies, Sarah thought it was a shame that she never got to write about the food itself, or the service or atmosphere, which many people would have loved to read about. So she set up her own website, A Lady of Leisure (www.aladyofleisure.com), to review the restaurants themselves, and has since branched out into writing about hotels, bars, holidays and all sorts of leisure destinations. Thousands of people a month now read and share her reviews.

- If your goal is to make a difference, launch a campaign. Paul Lancaster became so fed up with the huge number of emails he was getting that in 2011 he created No Email Day (#NoEmailDay), a one-day event to raise people's awareness of how much time is wasted dealing with emails. His big idea was that people should stop using email for 24 hours and use the time they saved to do something more productive. If they have to talk to someone, they should arrange to talk to them face to face or by phone.

Paul says: "I realized that every time someone sends you an email they are actually giving you more work to do. Reading, replying, deleting, forwarding, filing or marking as junk all takes up valuable time, piling even more pressure on your already busy schedule. There are so many emails flying around every second of the day that it can sometimes feel like dealing with them is all that you're doing."

To get his idea out there, Paul wrote a nine-page manifesto setting out his plan and put it up on Slideshare, an online sharing platform, where so far more than 60,000 people have read it. The first No Email Day was held on 11.11.11 and it has been held every year since, each time on a memorable day which works for both UK and US date order. In 2015 it was held on 05.05.15 and the year before that on 04.04.14. Although initially aimed at individuals and small businesses, large firms such as Microsoft have now also become involved.

4. Get pitching

As well as telling people what you are doing, at some point you may also need to persuade them to get involved. Perhaps you want them to provide equipment or a venue, lend you money, work for you, sell something to you, buy something from you. You can't expect them to guess what you need, so you are going to have to tell them.

If you have never pitched an idea to anyone before, it can be quite daunting. The good news is whether you are pitching your idea by email, phone or in person, there are some things you can do to make the process less painful. And improve the chances of them saying yes. Here's how:

- **Always pitch to a real person.** Never send speculative proposals to generic job titles or departments because they will just be ignored. Find out who the right person is, then email them directly. If the organization won't divulge email addresses, try firstname.lastname@organization.com, or with the relevant country ending. If that bounces back, try it without the first dot, then try firstname@organization.com, then initial (no dot) lastname@organization.com, again with the relevant country ending.

- **Find the link.** If at all possible, never pitch to a total stranger. Before you contact them find something which links you, no matter how tenuous. You might have grown up in the same town, or support the same football team. You might both be left handed, or dyslexic. It is a big cold world out there and as a general rule people feel much safer and happier dealing with people they have a connection with. Which leads us on to:

- **Do your homework.** Know your audience and understand what interests them. Do some Googling, read their LinkedIn page and Wikipedia entries, and try to get a clear idea about what makes them tick. And know every detail of your project or venture so you can confidently answer any question about it. Your audience will want to feel reassured you really understand what you are doing.

- **Go to the top.** If you are pitching to an organization, find out who has the authority to say yes to your proposal and if possible deal directly with them. There is nothing more infuriating than delivering a heartfelt pitch, only for the person on the other side of the desk to confess they don't actually have the power to agree to your proposal.

- **Get your numbers right.** If you are asking for money, you will need to explain what you will do with it and why you will need it. But you will also need to explain what's in it for them. A return on their investment, publicity for themselves or their brand through sponsorship, the feel-good factor of contributing to a good cause, for example. Whatever it is, spell it out clearly. And make sure your numbers add up.

- **Explain why you are different.** The world is full of people with big ideas. What makes you special? What is it about you and your ambition which would make people want to help you, or work with you, or hire you, or promote you, or talk to you? Explain how you are different from all the other people with big ideas and why you will achieve your goal when others may not. The more facts, proof and evidence you can include, the better.

- **Get to the point – quickly.** People are busy and don't want to hear waffle. Ditch the small talk – and the PowerPoint presentation – and get on with it. They will most likely make a decision in the first 30 seconds of meeting you, or within the first paragraph of an email. Scary but true.

5. Jump in

Pressing the green button on your ambition is a bit like standing on the top diving board waiting to jump. You can do all the preparation in the world, know everything there is to know about diving, have a brilliant coach, have T-shirts printed with your name on them and a fantastic support team waiting for you on the ground. But at some point you are just going to have to take a step forward, throw yourself in, and hope for the best.

Jack Walker grew up in a working class neighbourhood of Glasgow and when he left school he got a job as a quantity surveyor for various construction companies. His job was to measure and value all elements of construction projects to make sure they were being completed on budget. He did well and by the time he was 27 he had a company car, pension scheme and mortgage.

But Jack loved singing as a hobby and dreamed of pursuing a career as an entertainer. So when he came third in a local talent contest in a nightclub at the age of 27, he plucked up the courage to quit his job.

He says: "It was a huge gamble. Where I lived, singing and dancing were just not something anyone did for a living. The entertainment industry was a different world; it was what you saw on television. But I just thought, to hell with it. The one thought that was persistently in my head was that if I didn't try to become an entertainer, I would be the most unhappy individual ever to cross anyone's path on a construction site. I didn't want to spend the rest of my life being bitter and twisted. I knew that if I didn't do it now, I probably never would."

Jack spent his prize money on a train ticket to London and within two days had got a job as a singer on a cruise ship. He spent three years on four different ships as the lead singer, entertaining the passengers in production shows. Then he got a job as a singer at Bally's, one of the biggest entertainment venues in Las Vegas.

He now lives in Las Vegas where he hosts and sings in variety shows. He was the compere for the *Folies Bergère* show for many years, and had his own show, *Jack Walker and Friends*. He also produces other entertainment acts including the McDonald Brothers from *The X Factor* television show.

He says: "Sometimes I can't believe I'm really here, doing this for a living. It really is a dream come true. When I get on stage I feel sheer joy. It is a huge thrill. I can't even think how to compare the joy of doing what I do now with what I left behind."

He is also earning many times more than he would have earned as a quantity surveyor. "Financially I am light years ahead and in terms of job satisfaction, you can't measure it."

Over to You

1. Spend a morning getting your social media presence up to date. Check especially that your profiles send out the right message, and that they are consistent.

2. Write a pitch and practise saying it to a group of supportive friends. Now get their feedback.

3. Send an email to someone about your project. Now.

"The way to get started is to quit talking and begin doing."

Walt Disney

11

Create a support team

"Piglet sidled up to Pooh from behind.
'Pooh!' he whispered. 'Yes, Piglet?'
'Nothing,' said Piglet, taking Pooh's paw.
'I just wanted to be sure of you.'"
AA Milne, Winnie-the-Pooh

The handwritten sign read: "Retreat for sale on the shore of Lake Atitlan, Guatemala – three houses and three cabins for $80,000. Fabulous views of the lake and volcanoes. Accommodates 12–20 people; very peaceful."

Deedle Ratcliffe and her boyfriend Mike were travelling through Central America on a year out from their jobs in London when they spotted the sign. They immediately went to see the retreat and realized it would be the perfect place to turn into a backpackers' hostel and diving school.

They had only planned to be in Guatemala for a few days before returning to the UK. But three days later they had bought the retreat, paying a small deposit with money left to Deedle by an aunt and arranging to pay the rest in instalments.

When Deedle – a childhood name that stuck – told her parents what she had done, her mother burst into tears. It was certainly not the kind of life they had envisaged for their daughter. Deedle grew up in London and attended boarding school before going to St. Andrew's University. Her father was an insurance broker at Lloyds of London and her mother was a magistrate.

They weren't any more reassured when Deedle took them to see the place she had bought. Her mother says: "My heart sank. It looked really flimsy; mostly soggy wood and bits of cane here and there."

Despite its idyllic setting, the retreat, known as La Iguana Perdida, was little more than a few huts set in a garden. There was no electricity, no telephone and no hot water. And the only way of getting to it was by small wooden boat from the other side of Lake Atitlan. Turning it into a backpacker's hostel was hard work, particularly as neither Deedle nor Mike had any experience of doing anything like this.

Indeed the first hurdle turned out to be their relationship, which did not survive. However Deedle stayed on alone. Despite enduring hurricanes, a rainy season which lasts six months a year and even an algae bloom in the lake, she has managed to transform La Iguana Perdida (www.laiguanaperdida.com) into a hugely popular hotel and backpackers hostel, described as "gorgeous and peaceful" by the Lonely Planet guide.

Despite their initial misgivings her parents have been incredibly supportive of her venture. In the first few years they flew out many times to help get the hostel up and running, Deedle's father often staying for weeks at a time. Her mother says that after the initial shock, it never occurred to her not to be there for her daughter: "I really felt that I didn't want to pour cold water on her plans. And a little bit of me thought, what a boring life I've led and what a wonderful thing to actually have the oomph to do something like this."

Deedle, who is now married and raising a family of her own at La Iguana Perdida, says: "Mum was very concerned I was doing this because I didn't love my family. It is only because I love my family so much that I am able to do this, because if everything goes wrong I know that I can just come running home."

No matter how ambitious you are to succeed, it can sometimes be hard to achieve goals on your own. Happily, you don't have to. There are a lot of people out there who will be happy to help you make it happen. In fact, every successful person has a team of people helping and supporting them. Think of all those heartfelt acceptance speeches at the Oscars. Even writing this book wouldn't have been possible without the help of a large number of people.

Here's how to find help when you need it:

1. Get your friends and family on board

The people closest to you are a vital factor in whether or not you achieve your ultimate goal. Their encouragement and support can be invaluable. So can their practical help, such as collecting your children from school, checking on elderly relatives, taking in parcels and answering the phone.

Indeed, you may find it useful to create an informal advice board of trusted friends and family to help you realize your ambition. Invite them round once a month and ask them for their thoughts on anything you need assistance with.

In order for all this to happen, however, you need to get your friends and family to understand why achieving your goal is so important to you. Without that they may resent the time you spend on trying to achieve it, which might otherwise be spent with them. So make them feel part of what you are doing. Explain to them what you are trying to achieve and why, and how long it is likely to take. Then, wherever possible, get them involved. If you want to open a restaurant, invite them round to sample your recipes. If you want to build a house, invite them to come location scouting with you.

This is particularly important if you have children. It can be all too easy for them to feel excluded and threatened by your ambition if all they see is your back as you head out of the door without them. If you are able to show them that achieving your ultimate goal can mean fun and excitement for them too, they will be your biggest fans ever.

Here's how to do it right:

- When you are physically with friends and family, be mentally with them too. Listen to what they are saying, and engage with what they are doing, rather than constantly checking your phone for messages, or making phone calls. This is not just for their benefit either. If you always feel that you should be somewhere else, doing something else, you will feel endlessly torn between different commitments.

- Draw up some ground rules that everyone is happy with.

- Make your goal their goal too. If you promise to buy a new games console for the family if you hit a certain milestone leading to your goal, you can be pretty sure they will do everything they can to help you achieve that milestone.

- Be aware of the sacrifices they are making. If pursuing your goal involves using family money, which had been earmarked for holidays find another way to make it up to them – take them swimming every weekend or help them build a go-kart in the garage.

■ Say thank you. Your family are likely to be the ones who are most affected by your decision to pursue your ambition. So show your appreciation, often.

2. Get a mentor

A mentor is an experienced and trusted advisor, someone who can guide and help you pursue your ambition. They can help you stay on track, provide a sounding board for your ideas, encourage you through the hard times and offer practical advice. A bit like a fairy godmother, really.

Many successful people have had mentors at various stages in their lives. Entrepreneur Sir Richard Branson had airline pioneer Sir Freddie Laker, inventor Sir James Dyson had his first boss, James Fry, and chef and restaurateur Gordon Ramsay had Michelin-starred chefs Albert and Michel Roux.

If your goal is career-oriented, there may be a formal mentoring programme you can join at work. If so, take advantage of it. The great thing about having a mentor within your workplace is that as they are higher up in the organization than you, they will be in a better position to hear about opportunities for you to progress, and may even champion you for the role. If you impress them, they may also tell everyone how great you are. The more people that know you and your strengths and abilities, the more likely your name will be discussed when interesting projects arise.

If your goal lies in a less structured environment, keep your ears open for people within the relevant field that you admire and whose opinion you would respect. Then get in touch with them to explain what you are trying to do, and ask them if they would be willing to give you some advice. Don't be too demanding and don't pester – few successful people can commit to a long-term mentoring role, but they may be willing to have a conversation for 30 minutes if they think they can be of assistance. Remember, the worst they can do is say no.

If they do agree to meet up, or have a chat on the phone, have your questions ready in advance, and take detailed notes of the conversation.

If you can't find a mentor this way, you may be able to find one through a mentoring website such as Horsesmouth (www.horsesmouth.co.uk) or Mentorsme (www.mentorsme.co.uk), a website which provides a searchable list of mentoring organizations for small businesses. In the UK, Shell Livewire (www.shell-livewire.org), the advice organization for young people, offers mentoring and the Prince's Trust (www.princes-trust.org.uk) runs a business-mentoring programme for unemployed people under 30.

Alternatively you might find a personal coach with extensive knowledge of the way a particular industry operates who would be happy to advise and guide you for a short time, in return for a fee.

Good mentoring clearly makes a difference. A survey looking into the usefulness of mentoring for small and medium-sized businesses found that having a mentor helped many firms achieve both a better and faster outcome than they would have done otherwise. The survey, which was commissioned by the Department of Business, Innovation and Skills and carried out by Warwick Business School in 2013, found that 49% of firms using a mentor said the mentor had helped them achieve a better outcome, while 36% said a mentor had helped them achieve a faster outcome.

3. Get in touch with former colleagues

If your ambition lies within the workplace, people who used to work there and left in happy circumstances can be a great source of advice and support. Particularly as they may be able to shed light on how the organization really works, who really makes the decisions and what schemes you may have overlooked. Best of all, as they have already left the organization they may feel able to speak more freely and honestly than if they were still working there.

If the organization you work for is an academic or educational one, you have an even better resource to tap into – the alumni association of former students or employees, through which you may be able to contact a raft of people happy to offer guidance.

4. Join a group

It can be wonderful to find yourself in the company of like-minded people. They are likely to have a good understanding of what you are doing and how you are feeling because they may well be doing and feeling it too. Even if you fundamentally like working alone, it can be fantastic to discover other equally ambitious people trying to achieve similar goals.

This is why people join slimming clubs, writing groups and running clubs; the collective motivation and energy of others can be an incredibly powerful force to tap into. Go online to see what is in your area, and if there is nothing relevant locally, join an online group instead.

One of the best ways to find like-minded people, and indeed mentors and people willing to give one-off advice, is by taking a short course in a relevant subject. Through the course you will meet the tutor running it and people who are taking the course, many of whom may be taking it for the same reasons you are, and afterwards you can all stay in touch and continue to support each other. Check out the suggestions in Chapter 2.

5. Get networking

A glass of warm white wine, illegible name badges and a roomful of people clutching business cards may not be your idea of a fun evening. Networking is, however, an unrivalled way of bringing you into contact with people that you may never have met otherwise, whether potential investors, business partners, advisors, suppliers or customers. Even though the internet has created lots of new ways to communicate, most people still feel a lot more comfortable establishing a working relationship with someone they have met in person.

Networking opportunities can take many different forms, depending on the industry. It might be a formal networking event expressly set up for people to get to know each other, or an informal networking moment at a conference or trade show – or even in the queue for a taxi on the way home.

Either way, it's the perfect opportunity to make connections you would not have otherwise made. So get stuck in. Here's how to do it effectively:

- Do your homework. Before attending a networking event, if possible, get in touch with the organizer to find out who has been invited. If there is someone on that list you would particularly like to talk to, email them before the event and arrange a time to meet there.

- Smile, act confident and look people in the eye. Don't interrupt conversations; wait to introduce yourself at an appropriate moment. And don't launch straight into talking about yourself and your project; ask about them first. If you can establish a connection with the person you are talking to – I read your book, I heard you speak at a conference last year – even better. Then keep it short, sharp and memorable.

- Give before you receive. Offer to put people in touch with someone you know who could be useful to their own project, or to send them a useful book, before wondering what they can do for you.

- Know when to move on. Don't get stuck talking to the same person, no matter how interesting they are. Leave the conversation by introducing them to someone else, or simply by saying "It was great to meet you, let's keep in touch". At a typical networking event you have a maximum of about 90 minutes to meet people, so aim to spend no more than ten minutes talking to one person.

- Follow up the interesting conversations with an email the next day to re-establish contact. Connect with them on LinkedIn and follow them on Twitter. Suggest coffee the next time they are in town. Email useful articles that might be of interest. Basically, stay in contact, even if there is no obvious reason to do so right now. Remember that networking is not just about meeting new people; it is also about staying in touch with the people you have already met.

The good news is there is unlikely to be a shortage of places in which to practise your networking skills. Most industries organize events for participants to get to know each other – your job is simply to track them down and bag an invite. If your ambitions lie within the technology industry you will be spoilt for choice, with the chance to attend several networking opportunities a day in London's Tech City alone. Check out Tech City news (www.techcitynews.com) for listings.

6. Beware negative influences

I used to see an old friend a lot, until I realized that every time I told him of my plans to do something interesting or ambitious, his response was always, "Oh, you will never manage to do that". Initially it was easy to laugh off, but if someone says that every time, to every idea you have, it can start to get a bit dispiriting. I eventually realized that his consistently negative response was really getting to me so I stopped telling him my plans, and inevitably I stopped spending much time with him either.

Take a moment to think about the people you spend time with. Are they upbeat, optimistic and supportive of your ambitions, or do they dismiss them and squash them down?

This is not about ignoring sensible constructive advice, or blocking out people who can point out any mistakes you make. It can be extremely useful to have constructive feedback from someone you trust. But if someone is always mocking or criticizing your ambitions, it can be really draining. Make a conscious decision to keep such people at a distance, or at least only see them in the company of more positive people, because otherwise you will never find the confidence and the courage to strive for your goal.

7. Learn how to help yourself

After the first wave of enthusiasm propels you out of the starting block, you may find yourself needing an extra boost of vitality half way round the track. This is entirely to be expected. No one can survive on excitement and adrenalin alone forever. Don't panic – now is the time to deploy your secret weapons to see you through the rest of your journey:

- **Stop trying to do everything yourself.** If you have stretched yourself too thin, then start getting other people involved, if need be paying them for the work they do. One good way to do this is hire some students on a casual hourly basis. If you can find students who are studying in your field they may even have a particular interest or skill in what you are doing. Put up a notice in your local college or further education centre.

- **Stop trying to be a perfectionist.** In most cases, good enough is good enough.

- **Give yourself space to think.** If you find thoughts going round and round in your head without anything being achieved, change the scenery. Do something completely different, preferably outdoors. Go running, go fishing, take the kids camping, climb a mountain. Fresh air and wide-open spaces can achieve amazing things and give you a real sense of perspective, proportion and possibility.

- **Identify any problems quickly.** Don't linger on with a situation in the hope it will somehow sort itself out. It rarely does, and while you are waiting for it to sort itself out, the problem may get worse. If something is not working, deal with it.

- **Think laterally.** There is more than one route to your ultimate goal. If your route is proving impassable, think about how you could approach the problem from a different angle.

- **Get reading.** Never underestimate the power of a good book or newspaper article to widen your outlook and bring in new thoughts and ideas. Philosophy, history and biographical books, even fiction, can all shed light on how others cope in trying situations.

- **Trust yourself.** Accept that sometimes there will be days when you simply can't remember why you are doing any of this. Why on earth are you stuck in your bedroom trying to write a novel when you could be sitting outside in the sunshine reading someone else's book with a cold drink in your hand? Why on earth are you halfway up a snowy mountain with aching legs and frostbite when you could be lying on a beach? When times like these hit, and they will, the secret is to stop analysing and just plough on regardless. Don't waste time and energy thinking about why you are doing it; you already made that decision, long ago, with a clear mind and clear head.

Trust your earlier self to have made the right decision. Just keep going and when your mind clears you will be glad you stayed on track. It turns out Winston Churchill never actually said his famous attributed quote: "If you are going through hell, keep going", but he should have.

Over to You

1. If you had a mentor, think about in which three key areas you would want their advice.

2. Consider who you socialize with – how do they make you feel? Do you usually leave their company feeling inspired or dejected?

3. Write a list of your potential support team – not just the obvious people, but others who you think might be willing and able to help you too.

"Keep away from people who belittle your ambitions. Small people always do that, but the really great make you feel that you, too, can become great."

Mark Twain

12

Eight ways to improve your chances of success

"Attitude is a little thing that makes a big difference."
Winston Churchill

S top reading for a moment. Take a few seconds to think about how great you are going to feel when you achieve your ultimate goal.

The fact is, you are going to feel brilliant. Thrilled, overjoyed, ecstatic. And possibly highly relieved and slightly disbelieving. The great news is that with ambition on your side, success is within your grasp. It really is. You CAN do this. Here are eight powerful ways to bring your ultimate goal even closer:

1. Stop worrying about what other people think

Myleene Klass has a postcard pinned to the mirror which was sent to her by a friend. It reads: Why the hell not? Myleene, who rose to fame after becoming a member of the pop group Hear'Say, says: "I see it whenever I am brushing my hair in the morning. Why the hell not give something a go? Because if you don't then someone else will. I look back at my career and I could never have imagined what I have achieved already. So now I think, why the hell not?"

Since Hear'Say split up, Myleene has built a successful career in music, fashion, television and business. This has so far included appearing in adverts for Marks and Spencer and Littlewoods, the clothes retailers, launching a range of baby clothes in partnership with Mothercare, presenting a radio show on Classic FM and taking part in the reality television show *I'm a Celebrity, Get Me Out of Here*. She now presents the television show *BBQ Champ*. In doing all these different things, however, Myleene has sometimes faced criticism and disapproval because she has not just stuck to succeeding in one particular field.

She says: "If you look a certain way or trained in a certain field, people don't like you stepping out of your designated box. But I learnt very quickly not to worry about what anyone else is saying to me. I am pretty fearless in my approach. I am very realistic and don't take criticism personally. I could have a million people say bad things about me but I have got an inner confidence that says, well actually when you are saying bad things about me you are just projecting your insecurities on to me. Because I am out there doing it."

She adds: "I don't aim low, I aim high every single time and to a lot of people I do aim unrealistically. But if I sat there crying about every criticism I have ever had, I wouldn't get anywhere. I would just go, you're right, I will just give up now, what shape doormat would you like me to be. I want to see how far I can push myself. I could just go and sit on an island in the Maldives, but I want to be like a sponge and suck everything I can from life. I don't want to ever say that I never tried."

Myleene says it is important not be intimidated or deterred by people who say you can't do something. She says: "At school my maths teacher told me, when you leave these school gates, we are never going to hear from you again. At music college they told us there was more chance of someone winning the lottery than there was of making it as a pop star. They were not great odds, but I wasn't going to just sit down and give up. That is just not innately in me, I couldn't do it. The drive is to keep on fulfilling and think wow, I achieved that."

2. Commit wholeheartedly to achieving your goal

Commit is a powerful word. With good reason. If you are half-hearted about achieving your ultimate goal, you are unlikely to achieve it, simply because you will give up at the first hurdle. If you are serious about being successful, you need to make a commitment to yourself to see your goal through to its conclusion. And you need to invest your energies into making it happen. In the days before everyone had mobile phones, a friend once bought an answering machine purely because he was waiting for a single phone call about a possible job and didn't want to miss it. It worked. The man called and left a message, and my friend got the job.

Claire Young was runner up on the UK version of the television show *The Apprentice*. She now runs her own business, School Speakers, a speaking agency which aims to inspire, motivate and educate young people in schools. Before she took part in the show, Claire worked for Superdrug, the retail chain, as a senior buyer. It was there that she got her nickname, Rottweiler, because of her determination to commit to a project and see it through. She initially hated her nickname.

She says: "At first I was like, oh no! But I decided that if I am going to be compared to a dog, I don't want to be a little poodle or a Jack Russell so I am actually quite happy being a Rottweiler."

The name stuck when she took part in *The Apprentice*. She says: "When I was called back into the boardroom five times, Alan Sugar said: 'She is like a bloody Rottweiler, she's clinging on to my ankles, whatever I throw at her, she is clinging on, she is not letting go.'"

Claire now uses her nickname to her advantage when working with young people. She says: "For me it is one of the best things because when I am working with students they can all identify with it. I tell them that if you are measuring the amount of drive you have, Rottweiler is at one end of the scale and at the other end you have got CBA – which stands for Can't Be Arsed. It is up to you where you want to be."

She says that a good way to commit yourself to a project is to say it out loud. She says: "I am vocal about being ambitious. I tell people what I want to do. I think once you've said it out loud, especially to an audience, you are committed."

3. Believe that this can work

If you are going to go to all the effort of attempting to achieve this goal, you should at least do yourself the courtesy of believing it can work. If not, why are you even bothering?

If you don't fundamentally believe that you will be successful, it will be really hard to persuade anyone else that you will be. This is not about jumping up and down shouting "I'm the greatest". But it is about consciously starting each day with a real sense of hope, positivity and optimism. It is about backing yourself to win. It is about giving yourself a chance.

The tragedy is that many people give up on themselves far too quickly. A recent survey by the Open University of 1000 employees about their careers found that 20% felt stuck in a rut, while a further 18% felt bored and demotivated. Another 11% were simply indifferent, and 8% said they had chosen the wrong career path. Just 15% rated themselves as happy.

If you don't have much confidence in your abilities and find it hard to believe you really can achieve your ultimate goal, there are three simple ways to sort this out:

- **Let the facts do the talking.** If you are one of those people who have bags of self-belief, fantastic. If you are not that sort of person, don't worry; all you need to do is focus on the facts instead. You may not believe you can become a concert pianist and sell out the Royal Albert Hall. But if you practise every day, in six months' time you will have already mastered the basics and be on the road to becoming a competent musician. You may not really believe you can become a bestselling fiction author. But if you write 500 words a day, then after 160 days you will have 80,000 words, more than enough for a book. You may not really believe you can cycle around the world. But if you start out pedalling in the right direction, you will get there. Believing you can do something certainly helps, but if you really find it too hard to do that, it doesn't matter. The facts will still get you there.

- **Think back to the things you have already achieved in your life.** Everyone has succeeded at something, even if it didn't make the front page of the local newspaper. You survived your first day at senior school. You got into the football team. You passed your driving test. You made a cake, which tasted great. You did it once – so you can do it again. The goal may be a lot bigger this time round but the process is still the same.

- **Fake it.** If you don't feel confident, there is no need to tell everyone, or for it to hold you back. Act confident and other people will believe it. And eventually you may even start to believe it yourself. Some people suffer from imposter syndrome – the feeling that you are not sufficiently knowledgeable or skilled enough to be doing whatever you are doing and are about to be found out at any minute. Perhaps the simplest way to deal with this is to realize that you are not alone. Many other people suffer from this too, and many of those people have gone on to become incredibly successful and to achieve their ultimate goals, despite feeling this way. So acknowledge it, feel it, and then get on with whatever you were doing anyway. You will be just fine.

4. Stop comparing yourself to other people

So she did it faster and he did it at a younger age. So what? You don't live their lives, you live yours. If you endlessly compare your achievements to those of other people you will feel terrible, and you will come unstuck. That's because there is ALWAYS someone who is going to be better at something than you. The great thing is, unless you are competing in the

400 metres race at the Olympic Games, then it doesn't actually matter.

Myleene Klass has got this right. She says: "I have never ever compared myself to what everybody else is doing. I am inspired by other people's fire, but have set my own crazy limit and I want to see what is the most that I can do, what is the furthest that I can push myself. I don't look at what anyone else is doing, and I think that is actually the secret to it. Because then I would be a second rate version of them, just doing a lesser version of what they are doing and not really achieving it. They would already have done something and I would just be trying to catch up."

Indeed, Myleene says you should never even compare yourself to her, because her public persona is only half the picture of the real person behind it. She says: "I'll be honest, I don't know if I could be friends with Myleene Klass, she must seem like a pain because her hair is perfect, her dress is perfect and her life is perfect. But it is not like that, it is just a perception."

5. Accept that you are going to make mistakes

Jamie Oliver reckons that he has messed up about 40% of the business ventures he has embarked on. Jamie first rose to fame through his television series *The Naked Chef* and has since amassed a personal fortune of £180 million from his television programmes, restaurants, books, FoodTube channel and other ventures. But speaking onstage at the Cannes Lions festival in 2015 about his business ventures, he said: "Some people think I am a businessman or massively strategic. I worked out the other day, I took a little review of my 17 years … I've wasted … about 40%."

He said that while the failures have been hard he tries to see them as research and development. He says: "That 40% is quite painful. But then I sit back and look at it – would I change anything? Did the mistakes not teach me powerful lessons?"

Indeed that is the key – mistakes are fine as long as you learn from them. Virgin has chalked up some great successes, most notably Virgin Atlantic, the airline. But reflecting on the failure of Virgin Cola on the Virgin website, the company's founder Richard Branson writes: "Declaring a soft drink war on Coke was madness. I consider our cola venture to be one of the biggest mistakes we ever made – but I still wouldn't change a thing."

He explains: "It was a great learning experience for our team, and in taking on the role of plucky underdog, Virgin seemed to win over a lot of the American public, which certainly made things easier when we launched subsequent businesses there, including our airline."

6. Don't let setbacks derail you

In 1922 Ernest Hemingway was in Switzerland, working as a correspondent for the Toronto Star. His wife, Hadley, had stayed behind in their flat in Paris because she was not feeling well. When Ernest wrote to her saying he had met Lincoln Steffens, a journalist and editor who wanted to see some of his writing, Hadley decided to surprise him by taking with her Ernest's manuscripts of his work when she travelled out to Geneva to meet him, so he could show them to Steffens. She packed everything Ernest had ever written – at that point a novel and several short stories – into a small case, adding in the back-up carbons too.

But while the train was still standing in the Gare de Lyon, Hadley went to buy water for the trip and left the case containing Ernest's work on the train. By the time she returned to her seat, it had gone. Although she and the conductor searched the train, the case could not be found and was never seen again. All of Ernest's work was lost, apart from a single short story he had sent to a magazine.

Many people would have been irrevocably crushed by such an experience. Some may have never even regained the will or energy to write again. But Hemingway was so determined to become a great writer that he put the loss behind him and got to work. He went on to produce enduring literary classics such as *For Whom The Bell Tolls* and *A Farewell to Arms*.

7. Act like you expect to succeed

One of the best pieces of advice I ever received was at the age of 25, when I gave up my relatively well-paid job as a reporter on a London newspaper to try my luck as a freelance foreign correspondent, known as a stringer, selling news stories and features to newspapers back home in the UK. It was a high-risk step to take – being freelance is a precarious way of life as you are only paid for the things you are commissioned to write, and even more so when you are trying to do it from a foreign country. There was no guarantee that I would find enough interesting things to write about for British newspapers – or that they would want me to write them rather than someone else. So when I said goodbye to the business editor on my last day in the office, I nervously joked that if the journalism thing didn't work out, I could always get a job in a bar. To my astonishment he suddenly got really cross and said, "Well if you think like that, don't even bother trying to be a foreign correspondent, because working in a bar is what you will end up doing."

His words stayed with me and he was right. When I was trying to get established as a freelance foreign correspondent there were many times when it would have been so much easier to simply give up and get a job in a bar instead. But I remembered what my editor had said and stayed focused on my ultimate goal. I didn't waste any time sightseeing – as soon as I arrived I immediately phoned the news desk of *The Times* and offered them a news story. When they said they would like it I had to type it out on a manual typewriter and fax it to them because I hadn't even got my computer working yet. I started pitching news and feature ideas to *The Times* every day, and when the news editors there realized they could trust me and rely on me I built up a working relationship with them. I ended up working as a freelance foreign correspondent for *The Times* and other newspapers for many years.

8. Take it one day at a time

No matter how enthusiastic you are, it can be hard to focus on a goal that is many months, or years, away. So focus on the next 24 hours instead. It is short enough to manage and yet long enough to do something significant. Think about how you can use today in the most productive way possible to get closer to what you want to achieve.

Over to You

1. Get a piece of paper and write WHY THE HELL NOT on it in big bold letters. Now stick it up on your mirror.

2. Buy a large paper calendar, pin it up in a prominent place at home and write down what you hope to achieve by the end of the week.

3. What one thing can you do TODAY to take you closer to your goal? You have until midnight. The clock starts now.

"If you think you can or if you think you can't – you're right."

Henry Ford

Conclusion

"The secret to getting ahead is getting started."
Mark Twain

I wrote much of this book in the café of my local leisure centre because builders were doing lots of drilling at my home and it was too hard to think straight. The leisure centre café is a favourite place for old people in the town to meet for a chat over coffee after they have had a swim. Which meant that I spent a lot of time overhearing their conversations. Somewhat to my surprise they did not talk about playing bridge and bowls or going on cruises, as I would have expected. Instead they talked about illness and death. The old people endlessly compared ailments, discussed other people's ailments, showed each other their ailments (feet, mostly), and talked about other people's deaths, all with a grim sense of resignation and inevitability. It would be their turn soon, and they knew it, and there was nothing they could do about it. As one lady said: "You know you are getting old when your entire social life consists of going to funerals."

All of which made me understand more clearly than ever that illness and death comes to us all. That there is no dodging it, and what's more, it is likely to be here sooner than we think. So whatever you want to do, get on with it.

Using your ambition to fulfil a significant goal is one of the most exciting things you can do in life. It makes you feel alive like nothing else can. But it comes with a "use by" date. So if you have got it, use it. Now.

Martin Roberts, presenter of the television show, *Homes Under the Hammer*, learnt early on the importance of not wasting time. He says: "At the age of 19 I worked in hospital radio and I would go around the wards and get record requests. There was one really sweet guy who told me he would give me three words that I had to live my life by – Do It Now. If there is one thing I try to do, it is that. Because the worst thing in the world is putting things off. Whether it is a scary thing, or a difficult thing, or just something that requires a lot of work, we all procrastinate. It is what we do as human beings. If we can get away without doing things till tomorrow, till next weekend, till after the weekend, till next year, then we will, because we don't like making decisions. But procrastination stops the majority of people being successful."

It can sometimes be hard to work out the best balance between now and later. Particularly as setting out to achieve a major goal may well involve short-term sacrifices to produce long-term rewards. But life is short. It is far too easy for the days and years to slip by and for "not now" to become "never". I just received an email from an old friend whose husband is dying of cancer. Gone are their long trips overseas and lively gatherings with friends. Her husband is now confined to bed 24 hours a day and the size of his life has shrunk to staring out of the window. One particular sentence from her email has stuck in my mind: "He wants to know how long he has left and the only answer he has managed to elicit is 'not years'."

Not fun.

Or as German theologian Martin Luther said: "How soon not now becomes never."

If you want an excuse not to get on with achieving your ultimate goal, there are plenty to choose from. Just listen to the people around you with big ideas and no real plans to ever turn them into action. Here, take your pick:

It's too hard

I don't have enough time

I don't have enough money

I don't know the right people

My friends would think I was mad/laugh at me

I need to look after my children/parents/dog

I need to wait until the house is painted

I'll do it next year

You too can choose one of the above if you'd like to, or make up a new one of your own. However, if you'd like to look back in a few years' time with a real sense of achievement, then there really is no time like the present for making the first move. After all, you bought this book. Or someone who knows you well bought it for you. Deep down, you already know that the time is right.

At the age of 37, Paul Lindley gave up his secure well-paid job as deputy managing director of Nickelodeon, the children's television channel, to start his own business making children's food. He called it Ella's Kitchen after his daughter.

It was a high-risk move. He had never run a business before, had no experience of the food industry and had remortgaged his house to raise the £200,000 he needed to get started.

Paul did, however, have a very clear sense that life is short. And he knew that if he was going to do something like this, he needed to get on with it. He says: "I had this fear of being at the end of my life and wishing I had done a load of things, and that I had nobody to blame but myself. I think the one thing that made me take the step from secure employment to the unknown world of entrepreneurship was the overwhelming feeling that I would regret it if I didn't do it."

Paul aimed high right from the start, focusing all his efforts on trying to get a supermarket to stock his products, rather than going for small sales in corner shops. That also meant he had to find suppliers who would be able to deal with substantial volumes if the business took off. It was nerve-wracking, but his bold strategy worked. Sainsbury agreed to stock his products even before he had made his first sale. The Ella's Kitchen brand was launched before Paul's self-imposed two-year launch deadline was up, selling a range of meals and snacks for babies and toddlers. It quickly established a strong following among parents and carers for its nutritious food and for its distinctive practical pouches, which could be resealed to minimize waste.

Eight years after launching his business, Paul sold Ella's Kitchen for US $103 million (£66.2 million) and remains actively involved. He has now set up a social business, The Key is E, and a children's organic bath products business Paddy's Bathroom, named after his son.

He says: "In my life I am ambitious to achieve things but I am very aware that I have got quite a short time to do that. I am 48 now so I'm sure I have less time forwards than I have had backwards. And there are still so many different things I want to do. I had better get on with it."

Still don't know how to get started? Try one of these, right now:

1. Pick up the phone

2. Send an email

3. Go to an event

4. Sign up for a course

5. Tell a friend what you want to do

6. Arrange an appointment with your boss

Yes, it really is that simple. To get a ball rolling you only need to give it a little nudge. One small but decisive action can make all the difference. It can be so easy to get overwhelmed about where to start your path to your ultimate goal, but if you do just one thing then you are already on your way. As the ancient Chinese philosopher Lao Tzu said: "A journey of a thousand miles begins with a single step." Or as the modern day version goes, the fulfilment of every ambition starts with a single email.

Remember that you already possess all the tools within you that you need to achieve your ultimate goal. All you need to do is plug them in and flick the switch to make them work.

Where better place to finish than with JK Rowling, whose Harry Potter books transformed her from an impoverished single parent living on state benefits to an international best-selling author with a personal fortune of £580 million. She has also donated millions of pounds to charity. In her commencement speech at Harvard University in 2008, JK Rowling said simply: "We do not need magic to transform our world. We carry all the power we need inside ourselves already."

I would love to hear from you – what your ultimate goals are, how you are making them happen, and how it feels to achieve them. You can contact me via Twitter on @rachelbridge100, by email on rachel@rachelbridge.com, or via my website www.rachelbridge.com.

About the author

Rachel Bridge is the author of five bestselling books about personal development, smart thinking and entrepreneurship, including *How to Make a Million before Lunch* and *How to Start a Business Without Any Money*. *Ambition* is her sixth book. She is the former Enterprise Editor of *The Sunday Times* and now writes for *The Times* and *The Telegraph*. She took a one-woman show to the Edinburgh Fringe comedy festival and has an MA degree in Economics from Cambridge University.

Acknowledgements

I would really like to thank all the people I interviewed for this book for generously sharing their thoughts and stories. I would also like to thank Robert Dudley, Holly Bennion and the wonderful team at Capstone for helping to turn an idea into reality. Finally, a big thank you to my family for their unwavering support, and an enormous hug to Jack and Harry for making every day brilliant.

Index

INDEX